Little One's Whisper

Little One's Whisper

ANNABEL IRIS ARCO

THE CHOIR PRESS

Copyright © 2022 Annabel Iris Arco

All rights reserved. No part of this publication may be reproduced or transmitted in any form or by any means, electronic or mechanical including photocopying, recording or any information storage or retrieval system, without prior permission in writing from the publishers.

The right of Annabel Iris Arco to be identified as the author of this work has been asserted by her in accordance with the Copyright, Designs and Patents Act 1988

First published in the United Kingdom in 2022 by
The Choir Press

ISBN 978-1-78963-240-8

Contents

Notes from the Author vi

1. Mamá 1
2. Nana Riah's Mantle 16
3. Annie Love 27
4. Snow Globe 35
5. Glass Skin 44
6. Snow Burial 63
7. Ice Dance 73
8. Snowdrops 85
9. Little Art 96
10. Shifting Shadows 105
11. Icy Surrender 117
12. The Bobsleigh Track 129
13. Growing Pains 142
14. Robin Bird 157
15. Raw War 164
16. Migrating Goose 176
17. Dolly 192
18. Rebirth 208

Acknowledgements 223

Notes from the Author

Thank you so much for picking up this book. Some names, some places and events have been changed, to keep my characters' identities a mystery. My book has not been written to point a finger. This not my job, my job is to simply heal. I wrote this book as someone once said to me you cannot fix people's pain. This comment troubled me. So, I decided to make myself a human hypothesis to this, to place myself back inside my mother's womb and revisit my grief, trauma and pain. With the help of therapy this became an organic journey, my therapist and I deliberately avoided inner child theories. I simply wanted to only use my raw emotions, a pen and tears. I hope *Little One's Whisper* touches you places, that were once untouched in me.

Love, Annabel

For you, for us, for them: throughout this book I refer to you, us and them, let me explain what I mean by this.

For you

You live in a grown-up world, maybe you wear a suit or high heels, aftershave or make-up. Yet how many of you will die as children? I believe true adulthood is pinned on greeting your own inner child, then nurturing him or her and reparenting that precious little one. There is a little one within us all. Maybe he or she never witnessed violence, or experienced childhood loss or abuse. Yet that little one is still there. Perhaps that little one was bullied at school, or never

Notes from the Author

felt good enough, or was pulled through a difficult divorce. Perhaps that little one longed for time with a distant father or was a care giver to an alcoholic mother. The examples are endless. I cannot help but believe there is a little one waiting to be hugged and healed. No one gets throughout childhood without pain. That pain finds a way to escape in the here and now. For most adults they die holding teddy bears in their subconscious, trying to soothe that part of them that aches in silence. If my whisper helps you recognise your own inner child pain, then every last drop of my pain has been worth it. As I began to write my book, my story with the help of my counsellor was an organic exercise. However, I am aware loosely that a theory exists known as the inner child theory. I did not research it and, therefore, I am not sure that my book links neatly or at all. For me it has never been about theory but about raw emotion. So, if you are looking for a neat theory then you will not find it here. I have not undertaken any research, and I chose not to edit my book. I wanted a raw expression, after all, pain is raw. This writing is imperfect, as life is imperfect.

For us (sister)

My darling sister Dolly, my darling Birth Mummy and me Little One. I raise my whisper for Dolly in your absence, Mum. I tried my best and I hope you can read books in heaven.

For them

For every child living in a snow globe, I want to see Northern Ireland and England follow Scotland and Wales by extending the 2019 Equal Protection from Assault Act and ban smacking. The British Government rejected on corporal

Notes from the Author

punishment as long as it did not leave bruises. Do they not see bruises are hard to find covered in clothes as skin is not made of glass? For every little one under any type of oppression, deprivation or in need. For every soul lost in this rat race and who is in need of being heard profoundly.

For the differently abled and elderly deserving of equality.

CHAPTER 1

Mamá

If losing a spouse makes life black and white, then I can only describe a baby losing their mother as suffocation.

Dear inner baby, please can I call you Little One? Little One squeezes my finger. Can I call myself Mummy, as I need to reparent you? Little One collapses further onto my arms. Some of the words I use will be too big for you to understand right now Little One. I will read this to you as often as you need it, so it absorbs into the very fibres of your being. I am so sorry it has taken me so long to write to you. I have been so busy looking at things from everyone else's eyes. I forgot about your view. This is neglect, please forgive me.

You fell into a mother's unconditional love with your mummy in her womb. You listened to her heartbeat, her laughter and her voice. Yet, Little One, it did not feel like home to you. You sensed the unrest, the chaos, the cancer within. You were only five pounds at birth, born with very dry skin, very pale eyes and wrinkled palms. I do not think you ever unclenched you fists in there. They are scarred for life with deep wrinkles. You monitored every beat and felt the pain of deep illness in neighbouring organs. You did not like it, darling. I know you felt it and will grow up to feel and sense things in a deeper way than anyone you know.

Mamá

I watch how you tuck your thumbs in to the palms of your hands at night to feel safe, you sleep on your tummy and not in the foetus position. You rub your feet together to soothe yourself, you take in every minute detail of your surroundings using all your senses. You learn survival techniques from conception and these skills will be needed for your journey Little One. Others will be empowered by your gift of being highly intuitive and sensitive. Try not to be angry with them, Little One. It is not their fault that they think this beautiful. I know you do not like this gift. It is OK not to like your present, only you will know that this gift has come with such a high price tag. The cost is immeasurable, but the gift is invaluable to society; I hope you grow to cherish it one day. You will grow up to want to help people so much but, darling, please be aware that some people do not want to try and mend their pain, they simply cannot face it. Be aware you cannot fix people all the time, but I wonder if you are brave enough to fully embrace your grief in all its forms. Then could your example shine light on their dark path and encourage them to independently step into freedom. Grief changes lives, it is earth-shattering, yet I wonder can grief be the beginning of a new journey?

Little One you have never fully embraced your grief, you have invested the pain in helping others, that is nice, but it is not biblical. We are called to "Love your neighbour as you love yourself", Mark 12:31, *New International Version*. Little One you have no full self to lay down, this stops now. The time has come for you to read your story and unleash your pain in full. Anyone can listen to your story, learn from it and grow as a result. However, be aware your story is too difficult for some people and it may result in future loss. I will not shield you from that, it is a reality. I want you to be brave and join me Little One, can we read this story together? I have crafted your story into a bedtime read for you. Our book is dusty, it has been shelved for 36 years Little One. We could choose easier reading options, but stories like ours are not supposed to be kept inside the body. We cannot wait any longer for the sake of you, us and them, let our story start with chapter one. Mamá.

I will explain the big words on our walks at the beach, I will repeat this over you daily until you know it word for word. Yet Little One, I want you to be emotionally literate above your age ability. A baby exposed to water can swim, a baby spoken to in dual languages is bilingual by the age of four; if this is so, I trust by the age of four you will be confident in entering dialogue with me beyond your years. I won't call a train a "choo choo". I won't call a bottle a "bo bo". I will call words to you in their fullness you will learn the melody and the rhythm. I know you do not trust me. I have not earned the right for you to feel safe with me. Yet I promise from today to do whatever it takes to protect you and keep you safe. I promise to do whatever it takes to release you even if I have to bend, break or bleed.

Mamá

*

Our Bedtime Story – Goodnight, Mamá

Dear Little One, your time with your birth mummy is coming to an end. You are beginning to sense her pain, decreased energy and unrest. I am so sorry Little One, I do not want to hurt you. I want to reach for a copy of *Peter Rabbit*. I cannot Little One, it is all happening so fast, the story is unfolding so quickly I can't stop. Your birth mummy is leaving Little One. I know you are used to see her leaving in uniform to go to work at the hospital. You know her workplace as you were born there. Little One she is not going to have another baby there, or do a night shift. She is crying, her breasts have so much milk left, you are hungry and sad. Yet tonight you had your last feed. Your birth mummy is not coming home, no weaning, no warning. No baby, your milk has stopped like a car screeching to emergency stop; your birth mummy took her last breath, sweetheart, she has gone. The same place you took your first breath when you were born is the same hospital she took her last breath on earth, but I believe the same day she took her first breath in heaven. The author of the bedtime story is called God. He has permitted these themes, people say that is because he is sovereign, I guess he must see the bigger picture over time. He communicates that to me often, but that does not mean it does not hurt. It is OK to hurt, sweetheart, it is OK to cry, it is not fair, I think we can argue death never seems fair. You have learnt this so young and it's OK not to like the story so far. You have lost the privilege of bonding further in your mother's love. I think you have also caught a condition known as a detachment disorder. Mummy needs to get you some help with this.

From today Little One, not only are we reading our story aloud for the first time, we are reading it and we have an audience, a big grown-up called Anne, a trained counsellor, is listening to each word. Do not be scared by this Little One. I have tried to share it in the past, but only now I have found someone whom I trust to fully share our intimate bedtime story. I know you feel abandoned and alone, may I remind you your birth mummy did not want to leave, she will always love you, she only left because of cancer, it is not your fault. Do you know her dying words Little One? They were, "Look after my precious children." Do you know how loving someone has to be to say that? Instead, her example points to Jesus. In his dying words he too was concerned about the suffering of his mother and told John to receive her as his own, John 19:27 "Here is your mother."

Daddy said life was black and white when she left, no colour; this is not your fault Little One. If losing a spouse makes life black and white, then I can only describe a baby losing her mother as suffocation. I am sorry, sweetheart, but I have to continue. Do you know, my baby girl, that every 22 minutes a child in the UK is taken into care? Their mummies and daddies have a

Mamá

choice, but often they choose to leave. People in government, big boys and girls there, are trying to find them homes; I do not think they try hard enough. They are too busy with other agendas. I don't understand what agenda could be more important than getting the basics right. Secure children grow into secure adults less likely to need government handouts, NHS intervention or the help of social services. Why, oh why is no one crying out for these innocent children? For the sake of you, us and them I will keep reading.

I wonder can our story help other people when we fully 'own' our healing? You should not have to feel grief so young; you will never know childhood innocence. You will always know grief alongside your toys, playing mummies and daddies will have no appeal. It is the hardest thing for me to close the door on the nursery tonight; you are crying for your birth mummy, and may I remind you that no matter how hard or long you cry she is not coming home. I ache for you and want to save you with all my heart, but I cannot sleep tight and I promise to give you Weetabix and milk in the morning I know you love this so much, you will grow up to always love this.

Daddy said you refused any artificial teats on your bottle; I think it is because you are trying to tell the world it hurts. This is your only protest and you do it well. From ten months you drink from a cup showing the pain is too raw, too real and too deep. I question God on his bedtime read Little One. Jesus himself questioned God in the Garden of Gethsemane. If he

Little One's Whisper

can wrestle with God over this then so can I. We could trade our story in for the *Mr Men and Little Miss* collection, or we could spend endless nights trying to find *Where's Wally?* Yet this is your story, please accept it can't be returned, swapped or edited.

You refuse a goodnight kiss on your forehead, that is OK Little One, I blew you thousands—I have sparkly glue and I will stick them on you while you sleep. Like the colours of the rainbow, if Disney's *Frozen* characters can lose their parents at sea and they can build a snowman and parade around the hall in grief then so can we. Did you know many of the Disney movies feature a dead, missing, or single parent?

I want you to explode in colour, I know you would prefer to hear *Twinkle, Twinkle, Little Star* tonight, but I am holding you in this struggle. Carrying your birth mummy around is too heavy for you. You will meet her in heaven one day and Jesus promised there will be no more tears there. I feel for you, but I want you to think of all the children bleeding today in the UK too. I am a teacher and I know education alone cannot fix them. Teachers now also need to be social workers, mentors, step-parents and comforters. Education is not enough, it is a lie to believe this, it is not a direct lie but a subtle deception. I do not want to subject you to the brutal reality of lies so young. But Little One you have already met the Fairy Godmother and Santa Claus. Please know that deception is normalised so young. Can you be brave enough to allow Mummy to teach you not to hide behind make-believe? Do not get me wrong, I want you to be full of imagination, I just want you to dream in colour and know how to distinguish between light and dark colours otherwise the palette of colour that can paint potential dreams can quickly be subjected to nightmares and villains.

You will see morning and walk your first steps alone soon. Those steps will be the first sign that you will grow despite the loss. I ache for you; I want to save you from this next chapter with all my heart. People think cutting the cocoon helps the butterfly, it does not, it kills it. It needs to learn to hold the tension of the cocoon. I cannot cut your cocoon and I do not have any plasters left. I have tried using plasters directly on your wounds for years and rub God on top like a lotion. Despite having all the head knowledge, practically, I have failed you. It should have been the other way around. God has the lotion inside my wound, plus my tears applied seven days per week. It will take time for me to get better at these reverse dressings. I won't qualify overnight.

You hear my words, but you do not like them, it is OK. Sadly, people do not fully understand that babies grieve, but I do. I have a PhD in it from the University of Experience, I have just been too busy trying to help hurting children elsewhere as a teacher. You did not go to the funeral Little One, I wonder if it was because you would be too noisy. You should have been invited Little One, this is not your fault. I know your birth mummy would have wanted you there, but you were left with a childminder called Grace. Not attending the funeral

Little One's Whisper

served only to support other people's emotional comfort. It sanitized the death. Aimed to reduce its sting. I wonder if seeing Little One the motherless, caused their faith to turn into action? The action from this day forward to commit to Daddy, their promise of continuous care into adulthood. Your soul was as fully formed as the oldest funeral attendee. Oh, the ignorance of being ageist in grief, your grief is valid. It is beyond valid. It is profound. If you had been granted the opportunity to have a voice at your mummy's funeral, I believe it would have been spoken in Spanish – the language of the soul.

Te estrano	I miss you
Te amo	I love you
Te quiero	I want you
Por favor no me dejes	Please don't leave me!

*

Daddy wants to read to you tonight Little One. He does not like our book. He is welcome to join us at any stage of our story. I cannot wait another night for him or anyone to come along. We must read aloud even if others are not ready. Daddy is only trying to protect you Little One, he loves you, but his love is broken by unresolved grief. Yet you cannot fix him, sweetheart, this is not your fault. I cannot read this story very well; I have never written a story before. Yet my desire to see you free forces my pen. It has been written on my heart

Mamá

for years, carved with a penknife at times. This story is raw, it's undiluted and it is simply my head, heart and soul uniting for your freedom. Mummy has to go to work and cannot write everything at once, please be patient. You spoke your first word today; it makes me laugh it was 'dirty'. Can we take your dirty cuts to Anne's house, she is like a doctor for the mind? Welcome her Little One, she understands our story is unique, I see it in her eyes. They are brown, you will grow up to know everyone's eye colour Little One. I think it is your gift from God to see things differently. I cannot fix you on my own any more, so I am inviting God into your wounds, and Anne. She listens, she isn't like the big girl at the church who didn't want to see you. It is a sad day when Church rejects a wounded baby.

When I first went to meet Anne, to check if it would be safe for me to take you there, I pulled the car over to stop at a public toilet. In that toilet, a child's foot appeared under the cubicle with lots of butterflies of the sole of her shoe. I knew in that moment, the butterflies on the sole were an image of the butterflies that God would imprint on your very soul. God chose Anne to help, this was beyond doubt a divine appointment. It cast my mind to the birth of Jesus in a stable. Only Jesus would turn up in a toilet. Please know you can tell me, or Anne, or God to pause and slow down. It is OK not to be able to rush. I want you to know you will grieve birth mummy's death as long as you have breath. Although, I refuse to allow you to paint it as the dominant colour of the fabric of your life. For the sake

Little One's Whisper

of you, for us, for them, Anne's house is in our routine now.

I cried writing to you today, I am not the perfect adult. I think it is healthy you watch me cry. Adults always try to protect children from tears instead of teaching them of their healing benefits. You do not need any more Calpol, darling, you need the salt of my tears to flush your wounds. Today I am going to hurt you for a minute Little One, Mummy needs to fit an IV drip into your hand. I know you will grow up to pull this out many times. But I trust you will allow God to replace it and surrender fully one day. The medicine that will now run through your veins is a pure intimate relationship with God and my tears; you need a full blood transfusion. It is OK, Little One, I am here, I have Weetabix ready for you and we can prepare a bubble bath for you and read the Ugly Duckling book for a treat. Tomorrow is a big day; I am going to get you your first pair of shoes. They will be red and you would not like them, Little One you do not like red or pink. I think it is because they remind you of the colours of love. You need these red shoes for the difficult steps to come. These shoes will always stretch and fit you. PS You will look pretty in red. For all conscious and subconscious neglect, I ask for your forgiveness.

Mummy has been taken poorly, interestingly in her womb – she might lose it. But I do promise to keep reading for you, for us, for them. Perhaps my womb is failing to open the womb of wider motherhood. I wonder is it because as each minute passes, another child in the UK is at risk of entering the care system. PS It is your fault that I am deeply in love with you.

Can we share our story Little One; these children in need require to read this story as much as you? Please stop feeling ashamed Little One as Mummy is very proud of you. You are very brave. I love you even though you still push me away, yet I know one day we will embrace. I pray as I close our bedtime read that healing will flow into you like a rainbow bursting through every blood vessel. I am here to hold you and nurse you into healing. As I am holding you now, I play in the background *A Mother's Prayer* by Celine Dion. Due to copyright, I cannot write out the lyrics, but I encourage you to listen if you wish.

You know the English language fluently now. I am also going to whisper Spanish to you. The Spanish culture is emotionally expressive, the language itself is soulful and passionate. But it is more than just the language, the nouns and adjectives, or the fact that Spanish words are gendered. It is more than the flavour of these words as they flow off the tongue in absolute delicate beauty. It is more than the list of words they use that capture emotions more accurately. I believe it is also how these words are delivered. They come with direct eye contact and tactile touches, they are punctuated with facial expressions and hand gestures. I once watched a grandmother take two hours to say goodbye to her granddaughter in Spain. It was not a 'take care now' exchange, rather a magical interchange of generational love and affection.

Little One's Whisper

The English language and its culture are often too stiff. We can learn so much from the Spanish language and culture in its warmth, its lyrical lullaby and poetic charm. That aside, it holds a depth that does not always translate with ease. 'Sobremesa' loosely translates as 'post-meal chat'. What I think it really means is that moment, that unique moment when the paella pan can wait to be washed. It is so big as it has fed the whole street. Still, the Fairy Liquid is not ordered to attention, no, why ever not? It is because sobremesa has taken dominance at the table, intimacy has organically arisen between father and son. The relatives chipping-in at times, even shouting over one another. Yet nothing unlocks the father's eye from the son's eye. The language did not need to be uttered. They stand to their feet and embrace. They cry forgiving tears in exchange for a fresh slate.

I do not believe that sobremesa is like our post-meal chat at all. Our post-meal conversation often dares not scratch the surface of anything deeper than polite. At times it brushes past current affairs and acknowledges the comfortable in this difficult life. Sobremesa calls for intimacy into the early hours of the morning. The pre-midnight hours are often playing the musical melody of the pattering of children's feet. After all, the Spanish do not seem to set children's bedtimes, they sleep and wake according to the rhythm of life. They have the freedom to be called into the late sobremesa too. Big ones and little ones lost in an overwhelming sense of belonging. This to me should be the definition of sobremesa. It is not post-dinner chat, it is a post-dinner connection that calls for stillness and reflection and, at times, debate splashed with angry undertones.

It is OK to treat emotions with equality, in doing so it can lead to conversation that encourages growth and even glimpses of the divine. Be proud of your English language, but do not allow your geographical location to stunt your opportunity to learn Little One. In my view the Spanish are masters in captivating love. I cannot think of Spanish culture and not smile. The Spanish word for smile is sonrisa. A sunrise is a smile on the beach calling you deeper and deeper into the ocean of embrace. Here is a kiss for your cheek Little One, the Spanish passion in me will leave two kisses as the English one-kiss farewell isn't enough for me, or you. Good night, my precious Little One, and good morning, precious readers, as I warmly welcome you into our story.

CHAPTER 2

Nana Riah's Mantle

Their love grows through their tears. I think Jesus likes it there, he is close to the broken hearted.

Little One I have spoken with you from conception, you know my voice and you understand most of my words. I can help you with the definitions of any big words. I now need you to enter into dialogue with me. Mummy does not want to let Anne hear your voice; this is not because she doesn't trust Anne, it is not because she does not value input and understanding, rather Mummy is aware that every human has their own grief story. Every human feels. Mummy told Anne that she can only empathise as it is her job. I do not believe that is the case. True empathy has to be experienced to be shared, perhaps not exactly in the same way but experienced all the same. I sense Anne has been wounded in similar grief places, and healed those wounds to become a counsellor.

I never planned to write a book; I only came here to get help with my OCD. My OCD did not manifest in common handwashing rituals fearing the contamination of germs. Rather my OCD is centred around the fear of loss, even the most minimal loss. I thought by coming here Anne would simply prescribe me a course of CBT, but instead she wants to dig into my heart. The pain paralyses my oral responses, so organically writing has become my vehicle of choice and subsequently a book has been born, as I now acknowledge you my little

Little One's Whisper

one and I could never tire of telling you how much I love you. You are my wee sweetheart.

Little One, can you tell me, now that you are you are a little older, about how you feel when you visit birth mummy's childhood house? Hi, Mummy, it is Little One. My speech is so good, thank you for teaching me so young. Are you ready to listen? Are you paying attention? Yes, Little One, I am all ears.

Nana's house is a detached old rustic cottage in the countryside, it has no upstairs. I think this is called a bungalow. It has been painted between the shades of country blue and teal green. The house seems to frown a little when I look at it. It sees a lot of Northern Irish rain and it is not sheltered from neighbouring houses. I cannot walk up Nana's long path. I always have to run or skip as the gravel stones creak and crunch beneath my tiny feet. Every pounding step seems to release the sweet smell of the wildflowers that line the path. There are lots of plants and flowers, but I have picked my favourite. I asked Nana the name of it and she said it was called a hydrangea. The blue ones in particular I love. They dominate her garden residence. I cannot contain myself the closer I get to the door jumping around in sheer delight. The gate is difficult to open, but nothing can deter me from the challenge to open it myself and reach that door. Nothing would hold me back, not the sound of the birds or the distance echo of children playing in the fields. Even the sound of the stream does not tempt me to play. Play can wait. I am just glad to be back home. I know I have my daddy's

Nana Riah's Mantle

house in the city, but daddy works a lot and I am passed around many houses. I find it exhausting. It should be everyone's birth right to have a home not a house.

When daddy is at home and not working, he is quite simply such a good dad. He reads me stories, and although he has a fiery temper he is also a man of fun. He does not have a controlling personality, and I know he loves my big sister and me. I also know he is broken from losing his wife. He receives very little help and has to pay for a cleaner, childminder and someone to do the ironing. His family and birth mummy's family live over an hour away by car. This leaves my daddy alone. He sometimes brings a girlfriend for dinner, but they never stay over. I am happy when he has friends come to play as I feel sorry for him. I really wish he was never left alone. It is so unfair and I guess I have learnt to keep a watchful eye out for him in his grief. His life is now lived in the negative world. Do you know what I mean by that, Mummy?

I am not quite sure I do, Little One? Well, Mummy, just look at an envelope of photos that you have collected after they were sent off to be developed. The main section of the envelope contains the coloured photos. Whereas, the minor section contains the strips of negatives, in black and white – there to be enlarged or duplicated. Negatives will degrade over time. I wish grown-ups would help my daddy to live his life back in colour mode. This is the 1980s so there is little social or financial intervention. I ache for him, he had to watch my birth mummy die. He had to have those conversations and watch her in pain. He had to let go of how his married life was supposed to be. A long life of love. Instead, he got three years with his soulmate in marriage. That is only, three winters, three autumns, three springs and three summers. Thanks, Daddy, for trying to do your best, when the best was not offered to you in this life. My daddy often calls himself Papá. He is and will always be my papá. The success and failures in his love towards me will never change the simple fact that I love him. I just wish he had of loved himself enough to get help with his loss. Te amo, Papá.

I need to go. I hear the whistling kettle through the window, the Aga oven always has a teapot on top. It is the Northern Irish way of saying hello and welcome. It does not stop at tea, there is always fruit loaf with real butter on it or wheaten bread with homemade jam. Mummy, I am only little, yet Nana has a china cup and saucer for me. I am allowed my very own cup of tea. I think it's Nana's best china, yet I am worthy of it.

The blue flowers surround the cup trim with gold, it is pretty yet understated. This china is not on ceremony, nor does it deserve special treatment in the eyes of Nana. I do not understand why people collect china and expensive ornaments to never enjoy them. They hide them away for a special day. Yet isn't every day with a loved one special? These cups have been washed in Nana's tears yet dried with her joy. Nana's kitchen table is long, my feet do not touch the floor, I swing my legs. I imagine I am a princess dining at a banquet in my very own castle. My castle does not need a drawbridge, there is nothing scary behind any of these doors, all children should never fear what lies behind a closed door in their home. When these doors open, I am met with an outpouring of sacrificial, unconditional and undiluted love. Even in the porch in winter the warmth can be felt. Nana teaches me about heaven, yet to me this is a piece of heaven on earth.

I am not very good at eating fruit so Nana squeezes oranges by hand; it takes three whole oranges to fill my glass. I do not know where she gets her patience, it seems to take such a long time. Nana knows I feel the cold more than most people, so after my nightly bubble bath she wraps me in a white fluffy towel and takes me to the fire to get dry. Mummy, I can dry myself now. Nana knows I cheat and forget about in between my toes, so at that point she insists on helping. After she dries them and sprinkles Johnson's baby talc in between them, she plays Little Miss Piggy on my toes and kisses them before carefully placing my feet in fluffy slippers. I cannot understand why she loves my feet. I think it is just because she loves me. I love her, I really, really love her. Nana is not a fusspot, she doesn't say I love you a lot, I think she likes to put love into action.

Mummy, I need to go, I have so much to do. I am always busy in the daytime here. I help Nana pick gooseberries and rhubarb, we collect peas in their pods and gather apples and potatoes, of course she has potatoes, what Northern Irish Nana wouldn't? Nana asked Grandad to build me a swing and slide, yet I wish they could just see that I am not in need of these gifts. I am fully content playing in the stream with my imagination. Or making perfume with flower petals mixed with water and pouring it into old empty milk bottles. I love climbing trees and making dens.

This is my wonderland. Nana does not like collecting the eggs from the chicken run, so I leave her inside with my big sister. I put my welly boots on and accompany Grandad to collect the eggs and the wood outdoors. Nana is often reading the newspaper and shows me pictures from around the world. All the while I keep my welly boots on just in case Grandad calls me outside to help.

I love colouring-in, Nana always has my colouring pencils sharpened for me arriving, although I must admit it is more fun when Aunt Annie arrives as she sneaks in felt-tip pens. Sometimes I fall asleep mesmerised by the fire. When I wake, with my welly boots now removed, Nana insists the fairies came in and did it. I think she knows what battles to fight. Nana told me that we are going to church tomorrow. I am not sure why as I see Nana has church every day, knelt in front of her fire reciting the Lord's Prayer. Nana gives me extra time at night to learn the Lord's Prayer, but I do not need practice time, I picked it up weeks ago I am just buying time with Nana by the fire.

I can say the whole Lord's Prayer off by heart, but what interests me more is what it means when you apply it to your life. I hope I know how to do that one day. The Lord's Prayer only has 63 words, Little One, above Mary Had a Little Lamb. Nana wanted you to know those 63 words above any rhyme.

Mummy, I wonder why Grandad does not let me sit beside him when he reads the Bible? Well, Little One, I think Grandad needs time to comprehend the loss of his only daughter. He is male, a provider and protector, and I think he feels powerless, broken and bereaved. Birth Mummy was the apple of his eye, he was bursting with pride over his beautiful, kind and caring daughter. A parent one day, not the next, well, not in active service at least. Unseen by the human eye, his father heart never stopped beating, it never stopped loving, it never died. Men are taught by society not to grieve, to be strong and hold it together. But who holds it together in death? I wonder where the pressure to perform in the hour of devastation originates, it is certainly not in the Bible. The shortest sentence there speaks clearly that "Jesus wept." I believe Grandad had no choice but to close the bedroom door as he read and grieved alone.

Men often find themselves alone in grief and this needs to change. Mummy, I sense his pain and I sense Nana's too, especially when she puts Oil of Olay on my dry skin. I think it belonged to birth Mummy as it's stored in her dressing table, with the application of this lotion it reminds me of my own unique grief.

Sometimes I see Nana and Grandad look sad sitting on their sofa as I come in from playing outside. I make a noise so they know I am there; I try to make them laugh and try to see if the chicken has laid more eggs.

Little One's Whisper

Grandad is always willing to check on the chickens. Mummy, can I tell you a secret? I really do not like these chickens, but I go because I really love Grandad. I wonder does he check on the chickens so much because he wants his missing chick back, his daughter. There is a void, a deep dark void, it cannot be replaced, it stings like a bee, caught in the palm of a child hard at play, it hurts in places that words cannot express.

Every day the music is played. The Bible is opened, and the laughter is loud. The baking commences, the love is shared. The table is laid. The bed linen fresh. Visitors come and go. The candles are lit, flowers are picked. The Sunday roast prepared. Church attendance remains. Their love grows through the tears. I think Jesus likes it there, he is close to the broken hearted. The fire crackles with Irish turf and timber as the Christmas-tree smell permeates. Nana and Grandad will have you for the Christmas holidays, Little One, they adore you and treat you to gifts. They are ready and waiting under the tree with shiny gold paper with red velvet bows. Yet you are more interested by the fact they have dedicated a whole shelf to you in their pantry. It is fully stocked with Weetabix, fig rolls, Pears soap, baby talc, ten pence mix-ups, Polo mints for church and lollipops to distract from the pain of a grazed knee.

Mummy, my grandparents are amazing. Yes, Little One, no one can deny their godly dedication and care. You have learned so much at Nana Riah's mantelpiece. Yet the word mantle is not just the word for a fire surround, another translation can mean baton. Little

One, when you grow up, never forget to share the baton of this mantel with others, both big and small, young and old.

Mummy, where did they get their strength? Little One, go to the dining table and look at the Constable picture and tell me what you see, it might help you to understand. I see a man sitting on the end of a boat by the river. He appears to be building a boat. I wonder, does he want to escape? There are lots of trees and all appears calm, but I wonder is it calm for this man? Although as we all know, pictures can paint a very different story than the daily reality of the painter. I wonder, though, did Nana and Grandad see through the picture, through their unconscious vision. The painter John Constable's wife died young leaving him alone to parent his young children. Nana told me often he never wore colour from this moment on, and any paintings he did after this were limited in the range of the colour palette. Thank God, Nana and Grandad made the conscious and deliberate decision to wear colour.

Come here, Little One, let me hold and comfort you. OK, Mummy, but let's make this hug quick. I want to go and make perfume. I call the perfume Rose Water. It is simply roses petals and water. Oh, Little One, I love your creativity. I am working on other perfumes, Mummy, Hold on to Hope is my next batch. The sweet smell of hope, the aroma of welcome. It is difficult for me to try and describe the smell, but I will try. It contains a mix of Nana's turf open fire. Her fresh bread, lavender petals, Pears soap, Oil of Olay and Johnson's baby talc. It also contains notes of fresh sea air and line-dried washing. Really, what I smell is love. An expensive cologne that money cannot buy and time cannot erode. I wonder is the base note the smell of my mummy? I feel happy spraying this perfume. Oh, I know there are more pleasant scents, but I must remember to spray Hold on to Hope as often as I can. Mummy, can you play with me? You seem to be very busy with playing hide and seek with OCD instead. I wish you would stop playing that.

Let me feel, parent my heart. Even when I am strong let me cry, let me scream out my pain at the beach at sunrise. Let me sit in Areas of Outstanding Natural Beauty, let me draw memories when I struggle to remember them. Let me nap when emotion drains me, let me dance and laugh and create. Hold me, nurse me and lift your eyes of theory, or research. Together we will intuitively heal. Trust your heart above your knowledge. Mummy, why do you supress me sub-consciously? Have you forgotten I have already looked deadly cancer in the eye in the womb? I am a fighter. Mummy you need to let go of me in time, I will become stronger than you. It is time for me to grow into my destiny. Thank you for loving me nana and grandad. Your love remains within me.

> Psalm 103:17 "But from everlasting to everlasting the Lord's love is with those who fear him, and his righteousness with his children's children."

CHAPTER 3

Annie Love

The world offers love through the eyes of champagne, in the pursuit of excess and exterior beauty; but I think deep down everyone is desperate for Annie love.

Mummy, Nana is growing weary and Auntie Annie often comes to stay and helps her to look after me. But more and more I am staying at Auntie Annie's house. I could describe the house in minute detail, but my fondest memories are outside her warm and inviting home. Auntie Annie takes me on lots of adventures, she cannot drive but that does not deter her from organising lifts, catching buses or trains, anything to ensure adventure. We go fishing and have picnics by the river. Auntie Annie loves the beach and she has now bought lots of sand and created my very own sand pit in the garden, and my paddling pool there acts as a very tame ocean. If no swimwear is to hand, she makes my vest and pants into bespoke swimwear.

Auntie Annie knows how much I love my home comforts. Her food is organic and home cooked; I even like Auntie Annie's salmon sandwiches despite disliking salmon. She can even perfect my Weetabix, somehow preventing it going soggy although it's with lashings of whole milk. Who needs Michelin stars when you have Annie's kitchen? Auntie Annie often joins me for outdoor lunches. We love to picnic. She, like Nana, has lots of hydrangeas in pastel shades of blue, purple and pink. The blue one is always my favourite. Auntie Annie

Annie Love

has a big heart, in fact, she is just a big kid. She is, and will always be, my best friend. The closest thing I know to having a real mother, and my love for her is impossible to pen. How can I describe it, Mummy?

Open your heart, Little One, and be honest. I am not going to tell you how to describe it. I do not want to put the words into your mouth. Love is a verb without being propelled by action, it remains a word spoken too freely, written carelessly on tokenistic texts and, as a direct result, is undermined. Then society takes this diluted and distorted love, communicates it and tells us how we should feel. Social media portrays love as perfection. Love is not perfect, life isn't perfect. Yet, Little One, images appear on Facebook, Instagram and Twitter portraying love in its pure form, hiding the imperfections. So, Little One, tell me how you describe Annie love based on this?

Well, Mummy, Auntie Annie's love to me, is like the sun blazing in my heart during high summer. What is most precious is Annie love is a choice, she is, in fact, only a great-aunt to me and does not have to love me this much. Her love requires vigilance, commitment, hard work and plenty of sacrifices. Annie does not buy me with love. She does buy me gifts but not to earn my love. Her love is new every morning, I do not dine on leftovers from the day before like so many children in the UK. She does not count the cost; this love is so real that I could cut it in half and still have too much. This gift of love is wrapped up in laughter, tied with honesty, sealed with a genuine spirit and presented with ease. Oh, Annie love is practical theology. It is not enhanced by material possessions, which only act as a void-filler at best. The price tag of this love is too costly for many, Mummy. Only the truly rich can afford it, the millionaires of a selfless heart. Part of my name is Ann and I am so proud to have part of her written on me, everyone needs Annie love. Love by selection, love at its highest calling, the love for the adopted child, the love for the wounded divorcee, the love of those in pain unable to return the favour. Oh, Annie love, it bursts out of my veins, it is free of control, totally free, no manipulation.

Interestingly, Auntie Annie is not as conventionally pretty as her female siblings, yet her inner beauty makes her the prettiest. It says in the Bible, "no beauty beheld Jesus", it is easy to love the pretty perfect things in life, sin seems sparkling. Satan himself has been described as beautiful. The world offers love through the eyes of champagne, in the pursuit of excess and exterior beauty; but I think deep down everyone is simply desperate for Annie love. Annie's love is not religious, but it is God-driven and whispers to the soul with lightness, laughter and hope. It is easy to love the pretty and the perfect things, but they are often not real. Well, you will be surprised to hear Annie is not without her own grief story. She knows grief, she has not lost her only child like her sister, my nana. Her grief is different all grief is ...

Grief is labelled, pigeon-holed and subjected to discrimination. I feel sorry for grief.

It just wants to be understood.

Annie Love

It is not the enemy; it is the price of love.

Grief and love are dance partners.

Yet we as a society prescribe set dance routines.

This is wrong, grief and love as dance partners should be free to dance unchoreographed.

Grief needs to be discussed often, if not daily then often.

Invite grief into your sobremesa, your home and even your Christmas celebrations. There is something about the nostalgic Christmas memories that arouses grief and yet, all too often, it is silenced by the noise of commercialism and Christmas cult movies. TV programmes have progressed so much, and yet millions of people tune in to watch the Queen give her broadcast. I wonder is this because they are hoping she voices not only hope, but the hardships of life. Perhaps, behind the tinsel and mince pies we rely on our monarch to touch on the pain, to permit us to feel, if even in silence, the sadness that is often present at Christmas.

No one pulls a Christmas cracker to reveal the suicide statistics at Christmas. No cracker contains an invitation for a lonely soul to share turkey. We put on our paper crowns and feast, while starving our emotions of the right to be voiced under the fresh aroma of the refreshing pine tree.

The closest dance that can accommodate all grief forms, is the flamenco dance. The dancer simultaneously expresses grief, anger, oppression and pain alongside relief, joy, liberation and grace. It is not scared to live in love and grief, it boldly displays the dance on stage. Each flicker of the fan, each click of the finger, each stomp of the foot, and movement of the body is a release of suppressed emotion. It is a solitary dance yet its partner is the audience – those clapping, playing the guitar and shouting "Bueno, Bueno." They stay in the present, they encourage the dance expression. No, this audience hold the dance in the present feeling the pleasure amidst the pain. They did not hide away in the hard bits offering hope of brighter tomorrows as a distraction. They do not reminisce over good memories to avoid the present pain. No, this audience hold the dance in the present. They allow pain and grief to move towards grace and hope, freely. Mummy, can you buy me a red dress, I need to dance flamenco? I do not need lessons, though, I think it will be inherent in me to dance this untaught. The waltz helps no one at this time. Grief stretches our heart muscles, grief should not isolate us Mummy, but unite us all in love, passion and belonging.

    Auntie Annie married later on in life; I wonder is this why she did not have her own biological children? Just because she did not bear her own flesh and blood offspring, this did not disqualify her from motherhood. Never ignore the sketch of a child, albeit in black and white, in the arms of a childless woman. Annie is a mother, my mother. Annie could have chosen bitterness and jealousy and not helped her nana with her granddaughters. Women are often displaced and shunned from the community of mothers when they are childless, this needs to stop. Miscarriage, infant death and infertility cannot rob a mother heart, all grief

Annie Love

is valid, whether tangibly held, or held in the arms of dreams in the basement of the longing heart.

Annie loses her dear husband after a short time in marital love, oh, the searing loss, the shattered life script and lifetime of further stigma surrounding widows. Do people not see, Sam is as real to her now as their wedding day? To others he lives in her china cabinet in a dusty photo frame. Yet to her, I believe he is present on Christmas morning and in her darkest hour. Mummy have I told you lately how much I love her? I only spend a few hours in my own bed at night as I come through to share Annie's bed. She is hard of hearing and keeps her alarm clock in a biscuit tin under her pillow. I know she cannot hear me come in before Nana's sunrise rule. But she chooses not to see the clock, or reject the touch of my hands, holding onto her as my knees press into her back. Oh, Annie love, it is an open door just like God's heart: 1 John 4:8 "Anyone who does not love, does not know God because God is love." Annie's love laughs, her house is filled with laughter as she collects love; moments from photos of her loved ones to shells from a fond beach trip, she treasures every drip of love.

Mummy, I am tired now and I need a nap. Before I go, let me leave me you with my favourite Annie love story. On one particular trip to the seaside, auntie Annie bought both my big sister and me hand puppets that squeaked. On the long bus ride home, I squeaked mine continually. The man sitting in front of us told my auntie Annie to get me to stop. She said in a firm tone,

Little One's Whisper

"She is a young child, without a mother, enjoying the simple pleasures of a new toy. She has experienced more pain than you may ever know in a lifetime, so if this puppet squeaks the whole way home, so be it."

As a result, the bus driver ushered Annie, my big sister, me and the two offending puppets off the bus. We laughed non-stop and called in for some fish and chips wrapped in old newspaper as we walked home. The residue smell of the sea air was soon overpowered by salt and vinegar and washed away with lemonade. I later enjoyed a hot bubble bath. Finished, of course, by our family tradition of Johnson's baby talc, Oil of Olay cream and fire-warmed pyjamas.

Auntie Annie does not kiss my toes. Maybe she does not like feet. That is OK. I know that she adores me. I know that I adore her, but I would not kiss her feet either. As I return Auntie Annie's hairbrush to her dressing table, I notice one of my crafted gifts to her proudly displayed. I do not speak of it, nor does she. There is no need for words in this moment. Her choice to replace an expensive china figurine declares you are loved. Auntie Annie reads me to sleep. I get lost in her gentle tones and I am hypnotised into relaxation as she gently laughs at the narrative. Closing the book, she says, "I love you, Little One."

I reply, "Te adoro, Annie". I adore you, Annie.

Annie, I go to sleep playing in my mind, *Annie's Song* by John Denver.

Mummy from here on in, we will not converse aloud. It is my story now.

CHAPTER 4

Snow Globe

*You have a decision tonight as the music of the
snow globe plays. To turn the globe upside
down with or without due care, being mindful
of the child in there.*

I am in a snow globe; the fire is out. I have never lived in a snow globe before now, oh I have tasted winter before, but this is my first snow globe property. Only snowflakes inside this globe, icicles between my toes. It is winter (the bride-to-be's birthday today, too), my world has been shaken upside down, my head is spinning. My world keeps turning. People look inside to me, yet I do not choose to see. Behind the flower-girl dress, and all the fuss. This is only surface stuff. My dress does not disguise my story, yet it is convenient not to read between the lines.

The palms of my hands remind me of my past, yet the basket of flowers distract the eye. No compassion, no understanding of my heart. A simple flower girl. No grief. No pain. I am having to learn to fight to keep my life. It is not about me, others relieved at this sad no-mummy story coming to an end. Yet, as long as I live, her story lives in my heart, I am all she made of me. I wear her smile, her hands, her care. Birth Mummy lives on each day in my soul and DNA.

Oh no, people are looking into my snow globe. Leave me alone, can't you see, I am not the child you want me to be? I cannot be that daughter. I have lived six years alone. Mummy sounds like a swear word to me. I have

Snow Globe

not used that word, or written it down, yet this woman picks up my snow globe a few times in the last six months and says, "I am marrying Daddy. Call me mummy now, at once."

It is too much, too soon, too fast. Help me, let me out. No one can hear me shout. The glass is thick, I am stuck. The wedding dinner is served and it is lukewarm. I only like my food very hot. I get confused at which fork to use. I am expected to be perfect on the wedding day, my snow globe is shaken up again. Snow, snow, snow. Shake, shake, shake. After dinner I can't even dance, I watch the children play, yet my childhood is a lifetime away. I never knew true childhood ease, but this brings a new disease. The forecast is set for future snow, yet how can I state that as a fact. After all, how I see the world is so rare. Would anyone get it, or even care? I scream in my head for it to slow down. God made me gifted to see, yet others outside my globe are controlling me.

I cannot buy more time, no matter how hard I try, the hours, the minutes keep passing by. I want my nana; my grandad and my auntie Annie to arrive. They are not present today. I sit on the stairs of the grand hotel. A shadow of who I used to be. Despite baby grief, I was being taught to be happy and free. I live in the shadow at the top of the stairs, assessing my surroundings and trying to understand how to pretend in real life rather than playing make-believe like any other child. I do it for love, I have a big heart. To make Daddy happy, I must play my part. Yet all I want is my birth

Little One's Whisper

mummy to come and carry me away. Take me to heaven and let me play.

It seems so unfair, inside I protest, I am only six years old and my life is a mess. I wish I was ignorant and could not see all the wisdom and knowledge inside of me. Birth mummy was very clever, very smart. Daddy is more practical and into art. His new bride is not like me. I see through the façade, despite her great musical flair. Who wants music, if you can't even care? Other people enjoy the singing and the alto. Yet I can hear a different pitch. It does not ring true; I just want my Nana Riah right now. The sound of her humming around the house. She taught me to be polite and I really try, but I can't help but wonder why?

How can Nana survive losing my mummy, her only child? I wonder how Nana is feeling tonight? I wonder do I sense her pain? I think I can hear the creak of the oak dressing table open, but the Oil of Olay will not cure it tonight. I wonder is her fire on, or is she out with the chickens for the first time. Anything would be better than a January, a New Year without a child she once held dear. Now, no granddaughters nearby. Baby talc and Oil of Olay in the drawers sealed now and forever more. Santa was given a new address this Christmas past. The void of no daughter is bitter and cold. Nana lasted 20 days from this night. I knew something was not right the last time I saw her in a hospital bed. My heart ached on the journey home. My nana, my life, my world, she is fading away if the truth be told. Why did the wedding have to be at this time?

Snow Globe

Just because of a birthday date, sometimes these things should simply wait.

Take me to the ocean, take me now. I wish I could escape this snow globe and run to the nearest beach in the sun. I need to be near the sound of the sea and have new strength poured into me. I am only young but feel so old. I am drowning in tears sealed deep within. My tear ducts act as powerful dams. If I cry too much in this snow globe I could drown. It is air-sealed, tight. Maybe I have sand in my heart that soaks up the pain, as I'm too gentle deep inside. I wonder does the sand soak up my heart as I have been so intuited since birth. I wish I didn't see the world as I do. I am scared and confused. Why have I drunk of love at dawn, then been crashed into love at dusk? It is the strongest turning of a tide known to man. Yet it is my life, it is in my plan. Stuck inside this snow globe now, what time is it? Can I come out? Break this glass and return to the pure shore. No, that life is over, it is no more.

Does this snow globe world not have a key? I try to say "Our Father, who art in heaven." Do prayers get answered inside a snow globe? Held in the hands of other's power? How can God break through that world? I feel inside it must all be my fault. Why did I survive cancer in the womb to then struggle in this snow globe land? These questions I ask, yet the answers never come. I feel so much pain, where is Annie love, that kind that comes from up above? PS I am only six. Yet a theologian I must become, if I do not want to forget my daily bread, the Ten Commandments and

Little One's Whisper

how I was fed. The love I remember is so profound. People go with the flow, but I can sense Annie love in a flash. I can see, do you not know?

How can you leave me in this dome? What time is it? I want to go home. Oh, that is right I have no home, I now live in a snow globe at six. This is making me feel sick. Shake, shake, shake, snow, snow, snow. From the top of the hotel's spiral stairs, I descend to a scene of birthday celebrations. So many people are there they stop and stare. I am handed a cake and helped to blow the candles out. But I would rather light them up again, rewind time and pause the rain.

I am made to sing, but I cannot sing. 'Happy Birthday Mummy' sounds so wrong. I think I could sing semi-stranger are you happy now that you have found your ring? No one could see the ring was put in my basket of flowers, it was not tied just inside. It simply fell out. I have never heard anyone shout with such rage; her father had to usher her inside. He tried to help her find the ring. There it was on the path without a scratch, yet my heart bore the scar. I knew this was the start of my new life. Full of chaos, drama and strife.

Daddy's carrying the cases to the fireplace of the hotel. I feel like cold; I feel like ice. In my silence, I scream a thousand words. Perhaps a million. Where am I sleeping tonight? My snow globe is shaking from side to side. But in a snow globe I have nowhere to hide. Like an adult wearing a child's mask, I know to stand tall and not cry, after all, I am not very selfish, not at all. This is the happiest I've seen Daddy look. For him, for

Snow Globe

love, I have to do the time inside this snow globe world of mine.

I stay at the bride's parents while the couple honeymoon in foreign lands. There is no pantry there containing my own shelf. No itchy blanket, no open fire. The house is very tidy and clean. It looks very nice, yet I would rather be in the fields with mice. Where are my welly boots? Can't I go home? What time is it? I bang on the glass of this snow globe world. Yet I know my voice would not be heard. My head, my heart and soul can feel the pain. Yet I can't express in words how I feel inside. I twist my hair and rub my feet. I need comfort. Nana stroke my brow. Where is my baby talc – I want it now?

I now have a new granny and grandad to add to the change; the snow keeps falling. It seems the shaking continues to everyone's delight. I am scared. I hold onto my glow-worm. It gives a dim light. It is all I feel is mine tonight – the worst for me, when the sun wakes up, is that is my time to feel the pain again. The drops of snow, the sound of rain. Over breakfast I dine with a smile. Yet my Weetabix is not there. I only like Weetabix. Is this too much to ask? I eat other cereal, but it is a task, the comfort of simple things has gone now too you see. Where's my Nana? Where is the Lord's Prayer? I know God is in this snow globe with me. Yet the abuse of free will and pick 'n' mix Bible verses take flight. Telling God what bits of the Bible are right. Do you not think God too wants his full truth to be heard?

At times the perfect world he had planned, is shaken

Little One's Whisper

and ruined too by the hands of man. Taking the Bible, highlighting the easy bits. Then following their God. Limited, reduced, finite, promise-breaker, unjust, at least in the picture frame of their making like my snow globe. This too needs breaking. Nana has slipped away, I remember watching her being drip fed, all alone in a hospital bed. My world is out of control. I ache. Nana's funeral comes and goes without honouring her song. Shake, shake, shake. Snow, snow, snow. The hydrangeas are weeping, curling up and hiding. They grieve too. It is cold. The house is being stripped now the honeymoon is over. The familiar oak wood, carpets and pictures of my birth mother are removed and replaced like it is a race. Victoria Plum paper on my wall is evaporating out of sight ... shake, snow, shake, snow. My tears begin to drip in slow motion. Does someone hold a magic potion? Bang, bang, knock, knock. What time is it? Can I go to a warmer land, out of the winter (not so wonderful) land? Nana, Nana, where have you gone? This is not dealt with ... I am forced to move on.

*

Before you lift the snow globe with a child inside, stop, think. Reduce your pride. I don't care if you have been hurt, abandoned, divorced, widowed and the rest. You are the adult. The child is not a sticking plaster. Tend first to your wounds, you have a duty to put their needs first. Get inside the snow globe, can you endure the

Snow Globe

shake? With no money, power, possessions or land to ease your stance, go back in, take a second glance. Tape your mouth, then allow strangers to shake your globe; are you free to dance? Of course, move on, if it is safe. Ski into new love as long as the child is allowed to play and you have left a window open in there. Not an avalanche at bay ... snowflakes come in sprinkles too you know. Never let a child feel trapped in the world of your making. The child belongs to God and should be free, to be everything they are destined to be.

You have a decision tonight as the music of the snow globe plays ... to turn the globe upside down with or without due care, being mindful of the child in there. If you choose the latter, beware. The shaking of this snow globe might come to a rest. But the hurt and pain inflicted by the hand at power will reign this minute, this day, this hour ... The tremors will arise throughout their life, long after their snow globe is out of sight. Stop. Think.

I pray for more shattered snow globes around the UK liberating dreams, hopes, freedom and play.

We must free children. Nosotras debemos liberar a los niño's.

CHAPTER 5

Glass Skin

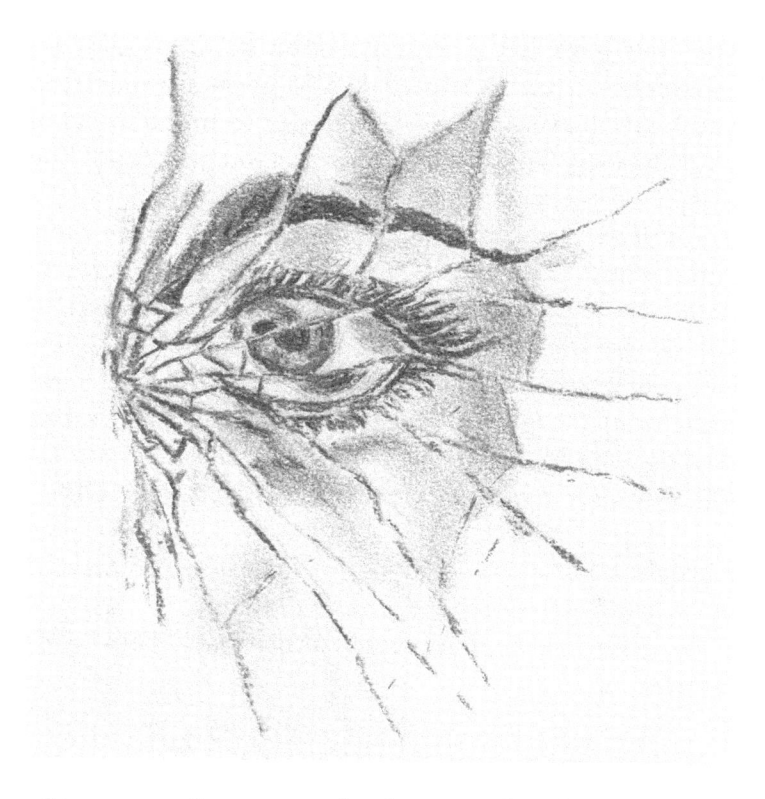

Everyone has wounds that need to be treated, albeit in different shapes and sizes.

I gaze out from the view of my snow globe sphere. I wish my skin was made of glass, people see into my snow globe home, but they cannot see past my skin. If only skin was glass, instead my body is wrapped in three human layers of skin. My snow globe sits on a shelf that reflects it in its best light. At a fleeting glance snow globes are pretty, delicate and serene. It seems fitting to live in this snow globe with a birthday in December. Yet I wonder how much more beautiful snow globes could be if they came with a sign that read: 'Please break glass in case of an emergency'.

You see, snow globes are adored items the world over, but they are also symbolic of entrapment. The stained glass of entrapment is as unique as the hand that formed it. You see, God didn't really make glass, did he? No, I believe he did not, glass is a man-made material. God made sand, lime and soda; man took these minerals heated them to scorching temperatures and glass was born. A clever chemical experiment yet, like many man-made inventions, glass is treated more carefully and honoured more than God.

God never intended me to live in this snow globe, or he would have clothed me in glass in the womb. I wonder how things would be different if our skin was made of glass? I wonder if it would be polished before the age of consent? Would it be cut, shattered and scratched? Oh God, why did you not make my skin glass? Why did you not choose opaque skin like that of fine, five denier women's tights that are barely seen by the human eye? I guess you trusted humanity with your choice. After all, your stars and sunrises are perfect. Skin is the largest organ in the body yet subjected to the most abuse; often simply by the very colour of it. We receive scans and X-rays to detect disease and broken bones, yet I believe our emotional pains are hidden away from such technology. After all, our emotions live in the soul. So, we apply a one-plaster-fits-all approach to emotional pain. This is not the answer.

Does no one see the uniqueness of the soul? That in itself is a problem as society tries to deny the existence of a soul as it's non-physical in presence with no fixed location in the body. The soul exists. If oil paints explode on canvases as each artist's soul beats. If music lights up the room containing a broken-hearted man with soul music, then how can you deny the existence of the soul? The soul exists even if not plugged into God. Each touch of tenderness, every warm embrace, each smile and glance of affection strengthen the soul. It invigorates the other organs and empowers the heart. To deny humanity of the existence of a soul empowers abuse of all descriptions and thickens the skin's exterior. No wonder so many people become so thick-skinned. My little hands press against the glass leaving my unique, damaged handprints behind. If you

Glass Skin

look closely enough you see skin trying to tell its story.

I, Little One, stand barefooted as I unravel each layer of my clothing. My battle armour of soft cotton. I strip back my skin like a coat and reveal my inner organs. I watch my organs work so miraculously; I am amazed at how special I am. A miracle. A true workmanship of God, my body now resembles a board game of Operation. I hold my bones and use my muscle and soft tissue to wrap my heart and soul up safely. The rest of me lies cold. I see the emotional pain entering each organ with force. The toxins do not have to reach the tear ducts as the other organs soak up the liquid trauma. This chemical cocktail of damage is so dangerous it would demand immediate medical care... if only skin was glass. Instead, this pain has no choice but to circulate my body in an anticlockwise direction – sometimes with no direction at all. You see, the body was not created to house such pain, after all, who would enter the house of God and damage the pews and stained-glass windows? The body is also a temple of God 24/7 and 365 days of the year, so is it not worthy of the same honour and respect?

*

The hidden trauma hides in every crevice and pore. You see, Hands has moved into my snow house, my dads new wife. My skin tries to comply to her hands yet how can skin comply with violence? Violence does not follow rules. Especially hidden violence kept for moments alone. I do not remember when it started but I remember the eczema starting and my skin weeping blood. I wonder what I have done that was so bad? Is it because my skin smells of my mother? I am clever and I can see that Hands has emotional scars on her hands, so I try to fix her. Yet skin cannot fix skin, it can at best help point it in the right direction. Yet my innocence cannot comprehend this fully. I work hard to fix Hands – I just want to feel safe. Does not every child deserve to be safe? I must be horrible; it must be my fault. I speak out about the outbursts of Hands in action, yet daddy never sees Hands in action and the very idea of it causes his temper to progress to domestic violence towards Hands. This silences me.

When I find the courage to speak up, Hands threatens to leave, she tells me it is because of me. Hands keeps a blue leather suitcase she packs in the bottom of my wardrobe, like a deterrent of blue leather lurking as a reminder to keep quiet. I do not want her to leave, but I want to be safe. My skin is soft, and I accept that this is now normal. I wish there was one eruption in front of my dad, but this hurt is controlled. So, to avoid Hands leaving, which would hurt my dad, I get skilled at minimising the risks. I flatter, I massage Hands' ego, and try to get her to stay as everyone seems to leave me. I make less demands of daddy.

I ice skate every Saturday morning, I have become very social and have learned to skate in and out of other people's home for refuge. There are moments of extreme joy too. There are gifts, affection and remorse.

Glass Skin

There are moments of happiness and normality. Yet even in these moments I do not fully relax, the not knowing is hard. When will the next eruption be? It makes my skin tense, my skin fights for justice, for Annie love and freedom. Does no one see things through my eyes? I am not heard even when I speak. My hands bang on this glass in vain. I am scared. These moments find my pillow soaked in tears and I fall asleep exhausted from the release of emotion.

My mind flashes back to images outside my snow globe and I wish I could turn back time. Yet I awaken again, hopeful that today will be the day that the sun does not forget to shine. I am always hopeful, but I cannot control time or the weather. PS Never forget that no child controls the time or the temperature of their world.

It says in the Bible that God collects all our tears, I wonder if he has enough old jam jars for mine tonight. I hope God recycles as I fear he will run out of old jam jars. Not just for me, but for every child that cries themselves to sleep some nights. Surely, we can reduce the demand for jars by simply loving children above materialism, selfish interest, careless words and cruel deeds. I ponder the consistency of skin again. I think it is Adam and Eve's fault we have skin. Before sin entered the world, I wonder did skin exist in another form. A substance similar to glass? Like the imagery described in the Psalms showing Adam and Eve clothed in the light of God, before they sinned.

For me, for us, for them, I will expose my wounds.

After all, we all have wounds, don't we? Yet we tend to treat the word wound like it is an imposter. Everyone has wounds that need to be treated, albeit in different shapes and sizes. Yet in society, there is a tendency to minimise wounds by bathing them in a generic pool of shame and bandaging them in silence. Yet shame and secrecy are the most penetrating of all wounds. They concuss freedom and underline all subconscious thought. Without treating shame first, the other lesions magnify and ooze, bubble up spitting fire. The laceration of shame may not bear a physical scar, but scars are there beneath the surface. Believe me, the laceration of shame screams expose me to the air, speak of me from your mouth, hold me in community and drag the broken pieces to God fragment by fragment. Do not dilute my presence in Bio-Oil, no, allow me out, let my unblemished skin reside beside blemished skin. Both as beautiful as each other. The first in its purity and the second in its capacity to overcome. Wounds no longer dripping in shame but kneeling, rising, and standing on the shore of belonging. PS We all have wounds.

*

I am only a child so naturally I want to play. I would rather do anything but speak up if the truth be told. I could spend hours playing Pass the Parcel, but I am certain in the end the prize would be inadequate. I could play Guess Who? But it too would not satisfy me.

Glass Skin

I could have a pillow fight; I could shout and scream and lash out, yet I know my head would never rest on a pillow in blissful sleep. I want to be free to climb trees and minimise the anxiety that manifests itself in OCD as I try to Connect Four with my pain

So, try I must. I am lifting my Etch-a-Sketch and designing my future freedom. My intention in this quest is not to cause others pain; my desire is to simply live outside a snow globe. In fact, I hope one day anyone who has hurt my skin is freed from their wounds too. I would quite like everyone to have a non-snow globe home. That being said, I need to be courageous, as glass cannot be smashed without the likelihood of more cuts to my skin. Perhaps these cuts have the potential to create an opening for buried pain and grief to be released. Perhaps. This is my only motivation in speaking, the sole desire to see non-snow globe houses and villages pop up especially for the children, the vulnerable and the elderly –those who cannot make a choice of where they take their shoes off. They all deserve more than a snowflake carpet. I, Little One, too deserve a real, permanent love-filled home and not a dome. I deserve my very own open fire. If it is not too cheeky, I would really like an Aga cooker and a free-standing bath in there. Oh, and before I forget, I would really like an old Belfast sink too. I would share this home, I promise; I would bake, even if it was badly. I would make endless pots of tea and coffee, not instant coffee but freshly ground, finished with a dollop of cream. I would welcome visitors able bodied and differently abled, young and old. They would receive a warm welcome on one condition, that they leave their dirty shoes outside and come prepared with clean slippers.

It will take me time to recall these physical and emotional wounds. This is not because I cannot write quickly, I write using the ink stored in my heart and soul. This ink supply cannot be forced to refill my pen. Please be patient with me. It requires a deep drilling into my ink store to get it to flow. The pen I use needs rubbing together to be warmed. It would be easier to write in blood; a simple needle linked to fountain pen would suffice, but I use the liquid ink of the soul. It takes time to draw the soul fluid and store it into cartridges. This fluid will not decompose in time and turn brown, unlike blood which will. No, the soul is eternal and words from there will go beyond these pages. It is magic, it melts ice line by line. The cost of this task cannot be described. How do you articulate the process of sieving out the wreckage of the soul from the intimate beauty within? Then carefully mixing it in unique proportions and crafting it onto tear-drenched paper. As if that doesn't sound difficult enough, I then frame that piece of paper and hang it up for others to read, review and potentially criticise. I think it would be much easier to crawl into bed and unleash the silent pain in privacy with the only audience being the old wallpaper that will not dare utter a word in return, but willingly accept the incoherent words as nectar to the wallpaper of flowers, happy to absorb the hurt of its owner.

Glass Skin

As I impatiently wait on new ink supplies, I enjoy making Mr Frosty slushy drinks with the melted ice from previous writing. I add colours and flavours just how I like it and I don't forget to add a curly straw – the kind that can be washed and reused. I like to reduce my plastic requirements when possible. I blow bubbles into my drink and I think I can faintly hear Birth Mummy, Nana, Auntie Annie and Grandad lift their snow cups in the sky as their glasses clink together, raised up for me their Little One. I am certain the day we meet in heaven again they will not reject me. I think we will all drink slushy drinks and chat all night. They will say, "Stay, Little One, at home," or perhaps they will whisper in Spanish, "Mi Chiquita ama de casa."

I am giving butterfly kisses to the pen I hold. The fibres of the soul in there are very cold. I am so scared to voice the secrets sealed within, yet the pen needs to move across the pages now. I know this as my tears have flowed like never before. They are bouncing off my lap as I lift my pen to start this task. Yet it is so hard to open the wounds trapped within my dome of glass. Even when I try to sleep to find rest. Yet the words keep jumping on higher on my chest. I do not think my lungs can endure another night. The time has come to bring this pain into the light. I am trying now to allow my writing to follow a different flow, not for others but for my own soul. It is like a little one's lullaby and writing it like this seems to pacify. This rhythm is not the best, very unrehearsed and plainly dressed. I am sorry but I cannot look back, I need to keep moving so I do not lose sight of my guardian angel's footprints which are always one step ahead. I trust these tracks although I do not have any facts. My gut tells me she knows best. To lead me to where my next step should tread. If the truth be told I do not have a map. I just know brighter days shine outside this dome, and I will not give up until I have my own home.

I, Little One, seldom just think of me, yet I am too scared to raise my whisper to a slightly louder tone, so I hope these echoes are heard from my frozen microphone. If only skin was glass, I dare say again the world would be able to see hidden pain. Yet wounds live deep down inside, a bit like forgotten ice lollies on the freezer floor. Energy dripping away to keep these lollies buried. I think everyone needs to defrost their life from time to time. Inherited pain is passed down the family line, inherited pain is passed on more than houses and cash lump sums. This cycle is spinning round and round. This needs to come to a rest for the future of children that deserve the very best. Too often, children are viewed as lesser by those who required bigger hats and gloves. They carry a briefcase or a posh degree, thinking this holds the answer to a child's plea. Oh, seriously, do not be so blind and hide behind a duty of care. Duty is simply not enough for that child out there. I would love if the name child was replaced with my name 'Little One'. So, this title can afford them the same human rights as an adult. After all, the humanity of 'one' is the same. Why, oh why, show ageism in pain? I do not know what is wrong with grown-ups? They will not legalise marijuana in case it acts as a gateway to Class A drugs. If only these grown-ups would apply this same principle to the skin of a child. Even the UN has failed to change the law on smacking in this land. Yet still we await a reform on the act of the hand. Oh, I wonder how many adults follow the "no red marks" to the letter?

Rather like marijuana, this too can act as a gateway to abuse in many a home. Using the law to condone an act taken too far. Oh, does no one see? This really is not how discipline has to be. I think it is time all the adults grew up and modelled better examples for their little ones to follow. It has been proven that positive reinforcement works best, yet the swipe of a hand they say works best! If an adult was to hit an adult in the same way, there would be a cause for concern. Yet not for a little one who is just starting to learn. I do not recall the very first time Hands touched my skin. I am sure it has gone on before today, I have just hidden the memories far away.

*

I sit on the breakfast bar up high, trying to complete my homework task. It is very hard I must admit. I get given very hard words to learn, and reading every night. The books and words are so very dull, no imagination or insight. Just a task I must complete so I can collect another sticker tomorrow in school for doing well in my reading and tests. I do try to do my best. Hands does

Little One's Whisper

not show much patience with me, she wants me to do it quicker, but I am too young to go fast. After a while she has had enough. I pretend I am finished to calm her down, yet it is too late Hands' temper has snapped. She pulls me from the very high stool by my long dark hair to the floor and kicks me as I try to get up. I need to collect the clump of hair that rests on the floor of the kitchen now. I won't run away until I get every piece, after all, this hair belongs to me.

I climb upstairs, my head so sore, I run into my room and shut the door. I know she will follow me once she sees I did not eat the packed lunch she had packed. I don't often eat much of Hands' lunch, it seems so boring every day. It's OK as I know what I want and my best friend Catherine's mum packs me a lunch. I try to remind her when I go to play that I am not a vegetarian and prefer meat as the dominant filler. A lot can be said about how a sandwich is prepared. Catherine's mum always grates the cheese and we nibble away at these like mice. Her mum has five children of her own. Yet, she makes room for me to sleep over when I need to get away for a bit. Catherine even shares her single bed with me. I do not fully explain the terror in my home as I am not sure anyone would understand, yet they sense and show compassion to the feeling that all is not well for me. In their home I would rather be.

I hear Hands climb the stairs and I get ready to handle the next attack. This time I am caught off guard when my cheek is blown with one solid smack and I am shoved against the wall hurting my back. I close my eyes, cover my ears, she is screaming loudly and demands that I look at her. Why, I wonder, why, oh why? Who would want to look into those hazel eyes of disdain? I would rather keep my eyes closed, or look at a random stain. It allows me to escape from the present moment somehow and endure the horror. I don't know if all little ones are like me, but somehow my body has special power, it can go into off-mode for up to an hour. She has now walked off and slams the mahogany door, saying if you tell your daddy there will only be more.

I brush the clump of hair in my hand, I place it inside my ballerina jewellery box. I have so many bracelets and rings, I can hide my hair under this mass of sparkle. My hair is so dark it blends in with the base, no one will notice not even one trace. The ballerina spins around as the music plays, her life seems far removed from my snowy days. So, I slam the lid of the jewellery box shut, how dare she sing and dance so much, I want her to feel just like me. Quiet and alone in the dark, I am not lifting up the lid again today It is not fair that she is OK.

I get undressed and run myself a bath, I am going to the Girls' Brigade where we always have a laugh. I get dressed in my uniform and go down for my tea, acting as though nothing has happened as that is how she wants it to be. Hands says she is sorry and reaches out for a hug. I tighten my body as tight as I can this time, I look her squarely in the eye and say do not hug me I would rather die. I sit down to eat and take a few bites, but I do not like Irish stew with too much gravy, I like it dry with wheaten bread by the side. I leave the table and I don't care if it is rude as everyone knows I dislike Hands' food. She makes the most horrible meals I have ever had, no surprise as her recipes are devoid of real love and have too much anger and bitter salt. I am hungry after playing hockey, but I stick to my choice, after all, at Girls' Brigade I will get Smarties and pancakes, and for a kid that is simply à la carte. A meal full of sugar and colour, a culinary delight. Oh, I am looking forward to my feast tonight.

Hands wants a child who is always neat and clean. I feel in the way. I feel so stuck I wish I could be removed in a big snow truck. Hands even hits me when she is driving, she does not care, her rage is out of control. She can control it in church, around families' houses and in shops, she can control it when others visit. Yet when she is alone, she is simply free to bruise and batter me. I seldom speak of my bigger sister and one day you will understand why; for now accept she is gentler than I, so to avoid Hands hurting her skin as much, I become horrible to protect my sister's skin as best I can. This is deliberate, it is in my plan. I do not succeed every time as her hands are much bigger than mine. I know what to do to make Hands mad, so when I see her ready to go for the not so little one in sight, I try my best with all my might. I aim to control grown-ups to be well-behaved for me.

The damage caused by Hands at power, changes how I view the world this hour. I make a promise, at the age of nine, that no hands will every truly own mine. I make a decision that when I grow up, that I will keep my skin tight and locked up. I agree to give some people a secret key to my heart – my mind flashes back to my childminder, Grace. There were two open fires in her house; she prepared my favourite snack after school with glee – a banana sandwich, with sugar on top, with real butter and my own china cup. I always scored ten out of ten on homework completed in her care. I think this was because my intelligence was not put off by fear. She did not expect me to be perfect in every task. Grace's house was safe. My big sister enjoyed it there too. We played with Grace's little one called Dorothy. She was so very tiny and cute. Grace washed my uniform every night. At school I smelt Grace's house on my chest. It seemed to give me extra power and I read aloud in assembly very well as I felt her care lingered in the air.

This flashback now fills me with pain as this safety was removed from under my bare feet like a rug. Who needs a babysitter when you have now been given a mum? People get fixated with titles. They seem delighted that I can now use the word Mummy, but Grace settled my anxious tummy. Grace takes me to shows and to Mr McGee's sweet shop. Grace had compassion for my loss and shared her home with extra cost. I thank God for the memories of my childminder Grace, who did much more than necessary for the money exchanged in her hand. She showed God in all her ways, she gave me hope for future snowy days. She is no longer my childminder now but she holds the key to my heart, and I know when things get tougher down the track with Hands, as I suspect, I can arrive at her house, albeit as a guest, to recuperate before further unrest.

Hands has scars it is plain to see. I just wish she had treated them before handling me. I have good days in between all the strife, Hands really also knows how to be very nice. Hands can be good when she really tries, it is just she is battling issues too big for my life. There are strawberry milkshakes in town later today. Hands is taking me to a massive toy shop in town to pick whatever I would like. I know today won't contain the slightest rage, some days read a very different page. This is very confusing, I must confess, so up and down it creates a mess. Perhaps Hands only knows this life, perhaps she is repeating the tune in her mind as she never dealt with her own unconscious pain. This is a real shame. Mix this with all my daddy's hurts and it makes for a very sticky dessert.

Oh, there must be more to this life inside my snow globe. A world awaiting with new treasures to unfold. A world where little ones are totally free and not subjected to inherited pain like me. My memory now is starting to recall many other moments of physical pain. From being kicked down the stairs leaving a bruise on the back of my knee. Making me lie to Daddy even though it was plain to see a bruise to the back of my knee. I know one day will not silence me. I would go on my BMX bike today to get away, but my handlebars are bent. You see, I left it lying down on the driveway by mistake and Hands reversed her car over it. It was careless of me, I know. My skin is now hurting from this mistake, but surely there was a better way to say please store your bike carefully away.

It is difficult to sit in church today and watch Hands doing something very beautiful with her hands. She is one of the best pianists I have ever heard. Her touch on the piano is so soft and gentle, her hands really do carry potential. I must confess it doesn't match the theology I already hold dear. Nana never taught me about theology that spoke on fear, this isn't how God wants religion to be. Does no one else see this is it only me? Do not be too trusting of Hands on the basis of class, position or creed.

Violations exist in all walks of life, they could even be happening in your home tonight. I do not fully understand all the pain, I just know I must stay true to myself and carry the lessons from Nana's fireplace in my heart. You see she was never cruel, not even one bit, even though she buried her own daughter she kept her heart open to show God's love. I wonder, did she use her pain to fuel the flames of her fire higher, in her resolve to pass on down the family line a love so pure, so divine. It may even endure all this mess and one day liberate my mind and soul as the snow globe loses its grip. Oh, I hope so, even if it's drip by drip. I surrender my skin as a canvas to be tattooed. I choose the words in Spanish, of course. Decorating the font with butterflies in colour, and an equal coating of black and white ink to act as a reminder that black skin is equal to white.

Little One's Whisper

My tattoo reads...

Let my skin speak out for those too scared to whisper their wounds. Let my skin bleed for those who think that any abuse in society is acceptable. Let my skin bruise for those who have become too numb to feel. May my skin shed in protest for those whose winter night has lasted too long. Skin is not glass, so you need to take the time to see through each layer of it.

Skin is the largest organ in the body and screams out of its pores, stop hurting me! Caress my naked skin in kindness and respect. Kiss it better and let it breathe. Do not present skin as an illusion. We minimise the pain held in our skin to maximise how comfortable others feel in handling our pain. Offer your skin in raw honesty anyway. Our skin deserves to be heard, even if others do not want to listen. It has no voice, but it screams silently nonetheless. Shared humanity must be its voice.

For you, for us, for them, can we stop hurting skin?

CHAPTER 6

Snow Burial

I simply want to allow my soul to be naked on a page. Stripped of religion, of pride, titles or possessions.

I sit, I pace the floor. I stare out through the glass... sometimes I get angry and shout. Sometimes I am quiet. Not a peaceful, contented quiet, more of a numbness. I am frozen in anxiety and fighting my natural response to seal hurt. You see, naturally I want to rush away or fight other battles of worthy injustice – all the while ignoring my own inner war. I want to look for lost insignificant items I own in an attempt to bring a warm secure feeling within. Or, I could lose myself in hours of creative play tasks. I love to play; I ride my bike, I make dens and use my imagination to create new worlds. You see, life with Daddy and Hands is not always bad. I am never stopped when I want to go to play at other's houses, outside or in my many clubs. Yet I know one thing for sure: I have never expressed an interest in writing as a hobby. No, I am active, outgoing and sociable. Writing is a very lonely hobby. I am sure I could ski off to a writing club. Yet, I know I would only feel inadequate as they read sections of the published literary gems. This would hinder my writing, or worse still... stop it.

I do enjoy using a fountain pen and changing the cartridges. I enjoy making the strokes and curves of my joined handwriting look pretty. I love expressing art in how the words look. Yet the meaning of the content contained in those words is often far from pretty. The pain can be sensed in the intonation of my voice as I read the words aloud. These words present a challenge, and I know by evidencing these words on paper that I risk criticism and rejection if they are ever heard or read. You see this notebook is not locked. It is not private property like my Cabbage Patch Diary that has its own mini-padlock and key. I hide it in a shoebox. I hide little secret thoughts – from my ten-year-old innocent crushes, to a shopping list for my next midnight-feast party when I go and stay with my cousins, or friends. This is secret stuff when you are ten. Yet this open book has no key and padlock to keep it safe and protect my human desire for privacy. The desire we all have to build a secret garden within contained by walls for defences. Do you know how hard it is to then pick up a pen and hold that tension? Do you know how hard it is to do that alone? All the while having no guarantee of the end results?

I am lonely when I write. It's the loneliest hobby I have ever had. I don't know if anyone fully understands. Well, apart from butterflies. They have endured the tension of the cocoon. They have fully struggled to become butterflies. They understand me. I wonder do invisible butterflies flutter underneath my pen to support it. I wonder... you see, I need to get the pages to feel the damage of my wounded soul. The damage not only of the physical manifestation on my skin. No,

Little One's Whisper

that damage mixed with lashings of emotional beatings from the tongue. And the damage to my little eyes seeing Hands and Daddy's arguments often ending in violent outbursts.

It is ironic isn't it that grown-ups are obsessed with classification of films that little ones watch. I am ten and always insist I am ready to watch a 12-certified film. Sometimes I am allowed. The other times I am not I go to my friend's house as she has a big sister who sneaks us into her home-movie nights. Yet horrors, sometimes worse than the 18 classification are viewed by my little eyes. Oh, of course not only on the TV, but in real life, the film reel of my experience. Sometimes I do not see the images, just hear the words as I try to sleep. I hear the shouting and screaming. Not all little ones go to sleep straight away. I have a torch and sometimes I use some sleeping time to indulge in little one mischief.

My wounds are physically, emotionally and spiritually oppressed. My little body is sore, my eyes hurt. But my soul, it bleeds silent blood and cries silent tears. I want to invite these pages to soak up the pain. The ink of my soul is no longer adequate. The pressure has snowballed and my tender soul is bleeding. I can't restrict my soul to one organ. No, the soul inhabits every facet of the body. So, to stop the blood, I must compress the pain. I suck my soul out of every crevasse and I simply bury it beneath the snow. Oh, I take it out from time to time to hug it, to dance with it and enjoy holidays and fun. Yet I dissociate from it in frequent snow-burial rituals when I sense both perceived and real danger. Yet this is the scariest decision I have ever made, to dig up my soul from beneath the snow and try to mend it, chapter by chapter without placing it in the snow again. You see my soul is not free. It is too ill to walk, let alone fly away.

I nurse my bleeding soul in the odd church visit, on moments at the beach, in art and music. In memories of Anne's love and Nana's fire. It helps my soul, but the wound is infected after all the time left untreated. I need to let the blood drip until my words run dry. Not knowing how long that will take. I am not very patient. I have yet to meet another little one who is. I reduce my vocal pitch to a mere whisper, Little One's whisper. Can you hear me? My soul hurts. I want my mummy to kiss it better. Mummy I can hear you; can you hear me in heaven? I made a big mistake. I tried to fix my soul by burying it. This has caused a lot of mess. I just wanted the pain to stop. I am sorry, I hope you can forgive me for making such a mess with the gift of life you gave.

*

Now I see that the soul was never designed to ever be buried beneath snow; under the compressed hurts of impacted snow layers, isolated from connections. I wonder, was the soul never meant to be buried, not even in death. The soul is not sealed in the body, inside a sealed coffin, beneath six feet of soil and sealed with a gravestone. No, it escapes. It lives through the fire of cremation too. You see even in death the soul aches for connection! Naturally it is attracted to other souls. Either in the heavenly realm or through a connection to the lost souls who rejected God on earth the world over. You see, instead of burying pain, society needs to learn to face it in the fabric of life's experiences. In the Book of Psalms in the Bible, hallelujah is often used to introduce and conclude a poem. Every emotion is hung between these two hallelujahs. The Psalms do not just value the good bits, the bits we are happy to share over superficial chats and nibbles, the bits we feel safe to reveal. The bits on Facebook that say, "It is well with my soul!" Is it?

Do you need to share those moments if you are fully present in them? Fully connected to that unique time, place and companionship? No, the Psalms is the opposite of Facebook and social media and social pretence. Everything is shared between the first and second hallelujah.

The glory, the loss.

The success, the sorrow.

Birth and deaths.

Laughter and tears.

The eternal and the temporal.

This is a true presentation of our lives. I like the Book of Psalms.

I ponder the words of the well-known song, by Cohen; *Hallelujah*. Little One's journey is a cold and it is a broken hallelujah. Isn't that true for all of us through the course of life? The connection here is not limited to major and minor chords of music. No, it suggests the major and minor moments of life. The extreme, the mundane, the lowest points and the moments of awe and wonder. After all, we live in a broken world and only taste love and pure delight in heaven, the true home of the soul. Souls on earth are singing a cold and broken hallelujah, I'm scared. Shake, shake, shake. Snow, snow, snow.

Yet if I don't move my pen, my soul will forever be buried beneath the snow. My soul needs to be free; I can't live like this any more. Like a caterpillar struggles in its cocoon. My soul, too, struggles to emerge and transform. I do have support, but I have to own my struggle. Hugs are welcomed on my terms, practical home-cooked comforting food accepted, yet the struggle needs to be fully mine. If the truth be told, I'm not sure how to fix my soul. I just know it's a journey I need to take in my hope to escape my snow dome existence. I am good at lots of things. Yet I don't know how to write. I don't have any qualifications. I don't even have any spare time to educate myself on the rules of prose. No, I simply want to allow my soul to be naked on a page. Stripped of religion, of pride, titles or possessions. I am no one when I write. I'm just Little One. I think God is happy about that. In fact, the Bible tells me so. I was not previously aware that Little One was a biblical term. This makes me feel very special. Matthew 18:10 "See that you do not despise one of these little ones. For I tell you that their angels in heaven always see the face of my Father."

Little ones are taught by society to emotionally

Little One's Whisper

conform to suppressing pain. It's so natural for really little ones to cry. To scream and reveal their feelings of sadness while moving quickly onto future moments of joy. They instinctively understand the word hallelujah. They know that to embrace love and life in its fullest. It requires a full embrace and acknowledgement of the highs and the lows. I am conditioned not to do this. So, to help this process, I've decided to read my writing from a little stool. I read it out loud. Line by line, word by word to one other soul. I wonder sometimes, what if I am reading *Little One's Whisper* first to perhaps one day encourage other little ones to express their sealed hurts?

Perhaps there is a little one in us all. Standing in their unique snow globe enduring the fall of their unique snowflakes and longing. If even a silent soul longing for release. Pain is released somehow – it doesn't just melt! Yet healthy release of pain can be obtained. That may not manifest through a pen. We are all unique. Yet with the correct embrace and the permission granted to let go and say it hurts here and here. Then the journey of healing can begin. Can't it? I wonder if we stood still for long enough in this chaotic and distracted world. Could we see little ones in all spheres of life, underneath adults wearing suits and having powerful jobs?

Who would do anything but address the sore little one within, who is pressing against the unique glass of sorrow leaving their hand prints, etched like a work of painful art? Perhaps their little one is healthy. Perhaps their world took on aspects of snow globe living as big ones. Perhaps the pain is restricted to certain emotions, times or places. Maybe it's restricted to divorce, grief, rejection, or isolation or financial struggles. Maybe it's multi-layered, complex and messy. Whichever way, I am sure in my bravest thoughts that there is a life awaiting that offers hope of healed emotions. Don't you see it? I know I see the world differently, but if you can't see it, imagine smashed snow globes all over the nation, as the heart and soul temperature are turned up in a true revelation of God's love for humanity. Though I have an intimate relationship with him, being totally real, I have never looked into the very eyes of God with a naked soul before. Nunca antes habia a los ojos de Dios con un alma desnuda.

I have tried to do that by sitting on my little stool. Yet even in that I've dodged that full intimacy. Upon receiving the gift of a footstool, I took an instant dislike to the off-white velvet finish on the fabric that rests on the little mahogany legs. So, I chose some tartan fabric to cover it up. I like tartan. Daddy and Hands take me to Scotland a lot, they are more relaxed on holidays. I find tartan beautiful. I guess that stool resembles my self-worth. I didn't like my life, so I covered it in tartan and buried it beneath anything I could, all in the hope that people would look at me the way they look at tartan. I wanted people to desire me, to stroke me like special tartan fabric. To marvel at the colour and beauty in me. I am not tartan though; I am not even Scottish, it's not a transparent reflection.

Little One's Whisper

I, little one, need to strip tartan bandages off my skin, my heart and my soul, until it is lying naked in front of God, my inner circle and myself. This is easier said than done as all the while my living conditions are extreme. My world is still being shaken, the snow keeps falling and avalanches lurk behind mountains. It helps to read it aloud to Anne, not because of her qualification – I do not like theories – no, it helps because her soul is good. God helped guide me to Anne's house by providing me with the sole of a little girl's shoe covered in butterflies, it's only now I see that sole can be spelt in two ways. I wonder was the sole of the shoe symbolic of a real soul that was covered in butterflies? I have no facts, but I feel this to be true.

I may only be little, but I have a big job ahead. I have built stairs and hideouts in my snow globe to conserve energy. So in between all the work I can take time out, when everything is still and quiet. When no one is looking, to sledge! Everyone should sledge in the snow. I am little, but I love giant-sized fun, empowered by non-alcoholic strawberry slushes. PS Never forget to make time for sledging and slushes. Dealing with emotional wounds is exhausting and it is OK to have fun. In fact, it is vital!

CHAPTER 7

Ice Dance

The snowflakes are still falling, but they are losing their sticking power.

I have dug up my soul from beneath the snow with determined resolve. It was so hard to break through 36 layers of snow. One layer for each year of my life. The snow was so compact and I am weary. My hands are tired. Yet my little hands are now left holding my soul, and my soul is not at peace. It wriggles around and I need to work hard to nurse it into a state of calm. Snow, snow, snow. Shake, shake, shake. Oh no! I have forgotten I live in a snow globe; how am I going to keep my soul naked? The snow keeps falling, my world keeps shaking as I write. I look at my soul, like a mother looks at her first newborn. How can I keep you naked? I really want to help you.

My mind longs for it, but I do not control my external living conditions. I pause in uncertainty within minutes my soul is now covered in a blanket of snow. I need to move to displace this blanket – even only one day at a time. I take a moment to pray for a thaw. A thaw that will one day heat my soul so much that it smashes through my snow dome home. If the White Witch in the *Chronicles of Narnia* lost her reign after 100 years of the long winter of snow and ice, then can I not have my Narnia melted too?

*

Ice Dance

The word for soul in Spanish is 'alma'. I think this word evokes an intimacy that the English language fails to do. From now on, my soul, 'mi alma', will be called Alma. She looks very Spanish, with a mop of jet-black hair and a delicate but glowing complexion, almost translucent in appearance. She must feel the cold like me, as she wears quite trendy stripy tights. Alma and I need to move, and quickly. I shake the blanket of snow off her and kiss her head. I am sorry I buried you in the snow, but will you play with me on the ice? In fact, will you dance with me Alma? I know you are bleeding, but I will look after you; I promise I will not bury you again when I get scared! Please dance with me on the ice.

Look, Alma, look. Look at all the other little ones dancing over there with their Almas, don't they look so happy? That could be us. Even better, we could lead the way for other little ones who had to bury their souls too! Look Alma, look over there! Look at those little ones who are dead behind their eyes; look Alma, their arms are cut, they are cutting them in emotional pain.

Look Alma. Will you dance with me? Alma looks at me, I look at her. Time stands still. We are locked into this moment. The lights of the arena dim, the spectators watching through the glass. We begin to touch; my hands intertwine into hers. We move together albeit rigid and stiff. I can show you how to dance on the ice, Alma. There are drops of blood on the ice, Alma, they are yours. They should not be there; can we dance through the pain, can we face it together? Pain needs to be faced Alma, I think the blood will stop one day, can we take the risk?

Do you believe, Alma? Do you believe there is a better life than snow? Oh Alma, there is a life better than snow I feel it. I have not seen it, but I feel it to be true. I have to be brutally honest with you Alma, this playtime is not very fun. The dance we need to do is controlled and manipulated. I did not have a choice over the routine Alma, the music and steps have been choreographed for me. Will you still move with me? It is not my fault; people tell me it is my fault! They say I am not very good. Do not believe them Alma. I do fidget and react badly sometimes, yet I am fighting against injustice and abuse of power in the only way I know how. I am fighting for you Alma. I am not a horrible little one.

The ice arena closes in like a snow globe. The background noise stops, the ice shop selling snow cones pulls down the shutters. The other skaters somehow know to leave the ice rink, it's you and me now. Shake, shake, shake. Snow, snow, snow, hold tight Alma. Look, you can wear my new, white leather ice boots; I will wear my old spare pair. I will tie them up for you. I am not a very good lace tier. No one has ever taught me, but I have managed it somehow myself.

Mirror my moves, Alma, follow my lead. Standing on my tippy-toes, I use the toe pick on the front of my blades to creep my way across the ice. Each pick provides more power and speed until I push off with my outer leg, with my other leg gliding on the ice. I continue this process, swapping each foot until I am striding across the ice. Go slow on the corners Alma. Hold my hand tight we need to spin. Do not let go Alma, just allow your blades to move. Look Alma, as we spin around in this axis motion your snow is falling off. The snowflakes are still falling, but they are losing their sticking power. Alma it is a mini moment of freedom. Don't you love it? I will show you how to skate backwards, use your hips Alma. Take small steps backwards. Point your toes inwards. Then make shapes, right, left, right, left. Look Alma, you are going backwards! Wow, Alma, wow! We will need to jump, Alma. You can use your toe pick to power you in the air, then land back on the other blade. Don't worry Alma, I will stay with you until you get it. You are a natural Alma. I wonder did you watch me skate from beneath the snow? I wonder did you sneak inside me on happy skates?

I have heard souls have special powers. I do not think this is your first skate Alma. Our connection needs work though Alma. We need to build our trust. Can I throw you in the air Alma? I will catch you! Oh Alma, you are so brave; one, two, three ... and I have got you. Alma, you can throw me up in the air if you want and catch me when you get stronger. You will know when you are ready, every skater does. Alma, before we begin you need to know how to stop. Both feet together in a V-shape. It is OK to stop if you need to, I will understand.

The music of our set routine begins. It's tightly timed

and controlled. Don't miss a beat Alma. Tiptoe with me, twist with me and now we are gliding across the entire surface of the rink. The surface of the ice now contains scrapes from our tracks. Our unique memory begins to unfold. The timing of our dance tightens further, the piano sounds tense. It's the unspoken aspect of Hands' reign. The rink space closes in. Shake, shake, shake. Snow, snow, snow.

Our thoughts are now spinning around with us in this axis. We are trying to micromanage every detail of our existence. Alma this routine will not be consistent. You will see that we have to keep pausing our feet for moments of relief, to face the reality moments of despair and no fluid consistency: move with me Alma, watch out, look out for the black ice. Anticipate every potential danger. I have tried to tell my daddy that Hands hits me when he is not there. Today she slapped my face. She slapped again and again and again, all because I said didn't think I would need a coat today. I do not think my daddy believes me. I am side-lined in my show on the ice. A part of my heart now closes off to Daddy. Jump, Alma, jump. We need to be more independent of him. Don't relax, keep moving, looking and spinning. I do not trust these grown-ups. The female one hurts me with her hands and Daddy hurts me with lack of presence and intervention. I wonder sometimes does he not take much time for me because I belong to Birth Mummy. I wish she did not die, but it is not my fault.

Daddy never comes to my sports day or takes me out

on my own, just him and me, not since he married Hands, unless he wants to talk about his marital struggles. Skate, Alma, skate. Can you throw me in the air Alma and hug me? Catch me Alma, I am only light! Daddy reads to me sometimes, but even that is less and less. He goes out a lot to play sport at night. When he arrives home from work, I watch out of my bedroom window as he sits in the car for 20 minutes. I don't think he wants to come in. Sometimes I go out to him and he play-fights with me, yet he never comes to me first. Never. Daddy is very good with words and is very tactile! Words and hugs do not mean much when I do not feel safe in my world. I cannot understand why he has allowed my world to be shaken up so much. I wonder is he too busy to fully notice, too caught up in his own interests, or too scared to face up to the reality now before him. Yet as a child none of these wonderings matter. The truth is, whatever the reason, I am lost and alone. That is why I buried you Alma, to dissociate from the pain.

Alma our dance is dangerous, and we need to go to the edge to hold on. It is like the innocence of childhood, with the bravery sown in dangerous games, is now over. The dangers of the ice are real. Very real. We are now skating in fear, anxiety and dread. Our jumping is not as high Alma. It is because of the emotional burdens on our shoulders. Hold tight to the edge Alma. Shake, shake, shake. Snow, snow, snow. Watch your timing Alma. The timing is crucial to our safety.

Little One's Whisper

You see when Hands is having one of her days, she hurts me even when Daddy is at home. Oh, she never touches my skin then, but she doesn't have too, the look of control in her eyes is enough. The lashings of her tongue. The verbal abuse. The demands on me to look and be perfect. Daddy sometimes says leave her alone, she is only a child. Yet that results in them arguing. Last night this argument got so bad, I got up out of bed and crept downstairs. I saw Daddy hit Hands and then he held her head over the kitchen tap. She will come for her suitcase now and it will be my fault. I run back upstairs and crawl in beside my sister, I wake her and I tell her we must be better for Hands. As much as I know what she does is wrong, I don't want to see her get hurt. Daddy never hits me, but he is trying to get her to stop hurting us. Doesn't he know as a grown-up that skin cannot fix skin? If only skin was glass everyone would know, and all could get help. Help does come, as the ambulance arrives. I later discover it will be the first and last time. Yet the damage is done. Not only is Hands hurt, I now can never tell Daddy anything – his wounds are too big. I will come up with a plan Alma, spin with me out of control, spin for now, hold tight Alma. Shake, shake, shake. Snow, snow, snow.

Creep across the ice with me Alma, we need to take the hits, the cruel words and quickly switch our feet when we can have fun. We can make the most fun away from time with them, Alma; we can stay out more. I think we should go and skate to Daddy's family when we can. We can stay in the country for weeks and we can have a break from this routine. Switch your feet quickly Alma, look at me Alma, sometimes the black ice is worse than the cracks in the ice. Sometimes I think it is easier to be physically hit than to be subjected to the emotional trauma inflicted by Hands in a way. The dance of appeasing becomes internal as her passive-aggressive sulking can last for weeks. Oh Alma, Hands has moved back into her parents' house for a while. Doesn't Daddy see this is not working? Instead, he continues to reduce his freedom to comply. They themselves are in their own dance of dysfunctional love.

Alma, follow me. Jump, please try harder. Please Alma, jump. Jump the minute she comes home and greet her. This greeting will make her feel wanted Alma. That will ease our day. Oh, I know skin cannot fix skin. But Alma we are dancing for survival now. Shake, shake, shake. Snow, snow, snow. I glide to the side at three ten every day at school and go to the toilets. Make sure your face and hands are clean, tidy up your uniform. The teacher will sometimes ask why I go to the toilet so near to the bell. Lie Alma, say it is because you drink lots of iced water. We need to jump off the ice as much as possible and accept every turn. I know you are bleeding, Alma, but try not to be off school when you are sick. My stomach often feels sore in her 'care'. Hands likes routine, pretend you feel well.

Alma you have stopped, are you OK? Come on Alma, I will carry you in this last lap of the ice. You have done so well to skate such a hard routine as a beginner.

Little One's Whisper

In fact, I will stop too. You know, Alma, I'm reading a bedtime book at the moment called *George's Marvellous Medicine* by Roald Dahl. He manages to make a potion that shrunk his nasty granny. I have tried my own version of *George's Marvellous Medicine*.

> I used Daddy's aftershave,
> Hands' perfume,
> Soap,
> Toothpaste,
> Bubble bath,
> And salt, but it did not work.

Alma. It did not work. It is OK Alma, look the lights are growing stronger, jump on my back. We are going on holiday in this last lap. Hands and Daddy are always better on holiday. I wonder is it because they are not in Mummy's house. We will skate to the theatre and go for nice meals. There will be laughs and games. You have just got to learn to switch your foot Alma, enjoy these days, we can't control when they will arrive so enjoy them when the music lightens. It will take practice Alma. Lots of practice to learn the complex dynamics. This is not a dance for little ones, but look we have made it to the end of this routine. The ice is scary Alma, but you know the only time I got badly hurt on the ice was when I forgot to take the plastic guards off my skating metal blades. The plastic on the ice caused me to fall badly. We faced this together. Blade scrapping was done. Pain can't be guarded. It just multiplies like bacteria.

Ice Dance

Look at all the tracks all over the ice rink, not a patch left unmarked, not every step can be accounted for word by word. Yet, we know the true depths of the interpretation of our own unique routine now. We know and God knows. Alma, one last request, can you hold my hand and skate with me to the kiss and cry area to get our mark from the judge? I think it is called the kiss and cry, because either skaters get lots of kisses for their beautiful performances, or they cry as they are told they didn't qualify. I wonder what God will have to say about our skate? I am going to ask him what to do with it, and you Alma. You are still bleeding. I feel God kissing us Alma, he really is. Yet I feel his tears too. This was not his planned routine for us and he is hurting too. I think God is cleaning the ice with the big ice-hoover machine. Look Alma, he is restoring it and clearing our marks off the ice. Like a fresh slate. Oh Alma, can I put you inside my skating top now as God has my hand? I feel him saying I need to dance through this chapter again. You can be inside my top next to my chest Alma, but this time my partner is Alma de Christo. The soul of Christ.

We will need to dance this through together, as his redeeming love begins to overpower the trauma and heal the memories. With the routine flowing like Spanish flamenco through all the emotions both good and bad. The sound of the Spanish guitar grows louder and freedom echoes across the arena. I hear God say again I will always provide a substitute, if you do not believe me Alma look at the Bible: "He heals the broken-hearted and binds up their wounds," Psalm 147 v 3.

It will take time Alma, we might have to do it lots of times. But I guess we have our whole lives. For you, for us, for them, thank you for skating with me. Rest Alma, sleep tight inside the warmth of my skin tonight. Your snow-burial bedtimes are over.

CHAPTER 8

Snowdrops

If a snowdrop can endure winter, do you not feel that you too can stand against all the odds?

Alma, I am tired from all the skating. I know I need to go over my routines, but I am just so weary. Please come with me to my den. Well, it is really just a portioned part of the garage. It is my den though. Daddy has put a TV in it for me and a computer game. Yet, I prefer to play make-believe most of the time. I have an old sofa and my Nana Riah's wedding china. I pretend there is a real fire in there, but it's not a real fire it's only an electric heater.

Alma, if you close your eyes, you can see the turf burning in your mind! Let's go, I need to rest. What will you do while I am asleep Alma? I will be beside you Little One. In fact, you can put your feet on my lap. I know that it is your favourite comfort to rub your feet especially against another soul. Thanks Alma, I am just so weary... I can't stay awake! I am so grateful that you replied to me Alma. I love communicating with you Little One. Remember not all communication requires words.

Breathing in and out, I allow my breathing to deepen, I cannot fight it, so I tuck My Little Ponies beside me and say to them what daddy says to me: "Night night, sleep tight, don't let the bed bugs bite. If they do, squeeze them tight and they won't come back another night." I think this rhyme is for very little ones. I wonder if it is because now I am fighting much scarier monsters than bed bugs, that this rhyme now appears so juvenile. With that closing thought I drift off to sleep to avoid my reality.

I am skating, I am really skating well in my vivid dreams, I am. I am pacing up and down trying to lose Alma in my snow globe. I want to help her. But helping her is hard. In my dreams I scream, leave me alone Alma. I just want to play with my friends, people see me with you and they do not call to play so much any more – you are taking up my recreation time. Go away Alma. I can't see Alma, but I feel her close.

I won't bury Alma again. I made a promise and, besides, I like her, it is just I am not liking her causing so many changes. The changes are hard. I am angry Alma, sad, lonely, hurting and annoyed. You see, the day I dug Alma up I was much stronger than today. My dream deepens, I lose all sense of surroundings.

Don't take my dog away Daddy. I need to say goodbye to my dog called Beso (Spanish for kisses). She has cancer. I screamed and shouted at Daddy not to do this, but he is not the type to verbally argue. He is angry at times, yet at life, not usually me. So, I stop speaking to him. Hands taught me this hurts people, yet Daddy seems oblivious. It is not natural for me to sulk and he is the same. I am running out of options.

I am dreaming, but this is reality escaping in sleep. In my final act of stopping him, I frantically emptied all the money out of my Ulster Bank iconic hippo money box.

Little One's Whisper

In fact, I am a Super Saver and have two hippos now. The bank gives you them to keep your pennies safe. I count the money and use the Yellow Pages to contact all the local vets. I am so happy, I have found a vet. I run downstairs to tell daddy I'm only £20 short and can I have a pocket money advance? He is kind, so I know he will give me the money. I always negotiate financial deals. As I run downstairs, I see daddy putting Beso in the car. I cannot unlock the front door, so I run to the back door and down the path. "Daddy, daddy, stop!" He drives off. I run after the car in hope he will be stopped at the junction. Yet as I turn the corner, I see his car has gone. Beso has gone. I did not say goodbye. I hate cancer. I hate him. Daddy cannot cope with death; normally I feel sorry for him but not tonight.

I watched him kick Beso last night when she barked and barked. I ran and pushed him away. Can't you see she is just in pain, daddy? It is not fair to hurt her I screamed. Realising what he had done, he left me to nurse her. I thought daddies were heroes; my daddy isn't. I had a feeling it could be my last cuddle with Beso. The odds are against me. I am 11 and have already lost:

My mum,
My nana,
My grandad,
My paternal grandparents,
My goldfish,
Why not my dog?

Snowdrops

Leave me Alma. Go away. I would rather push her away than risk losing her too. Don't you see I am scared? I do not want this dance routine, or this life. Look at the bouquet of flowers, presented at the kiss and cry. Snowdrops and weeds. I hate my flowers. I hate them. Other little ones my age have daisies and sunflowers, it is not fair!

Oh, I know, I should be grateful. Just not today. I am too mad. I rip the green ribbon off the plastic wrapping. I rip the flowers and weeds and jump on them with my blades. Go on, feel my pain. Part of me feels sorry for them, but why does no one feel sorry for me? I am sick of caring for everyone and everything! My world is black, yet when I blink, I see rainbows and butterflies even if only momentarily. I fall to my knees and sit down on the ice. Untying my ice boots and one by one I throw them as far from me as I can. Who am I kidding? I look at the glass protector surrounding the ice rink and see an ugly, horrible and unlovable Little One. Tears are now running down my face as I awake. Alma, Alma, help me. I have had a bad dream, typical, Alma has left. Everyone leaves me, but now even my own soul has gone!

Alma is that you? Yes, Little One it is me. I can hardly see you. Oh, Little One it is hard to see me. I think you are too distracted until now to notice that, unlike you, my skin is made of glass and when sprinkled in snow I almost disappear into the surroundings. You see Little One, you buried me beneath the snow and you thought you killed my feelings. Yet your whole life I have felt for

Little One's Whisper

you. We were physically separate, but it was you who numbed pain not me. I felt you dream and went to the kiss and cry to bring our flowers by the den, you need them. But Alma I have been so horrible to them and to you in my dream. I do not deserve them. I did not say you deserved them Little One, you need them, you need to learn to love your flowers. Every last one. You see, the snowdrops are blessings and the weeds are the hard times of life. Some of the weeds you have should have never happened, nor can be justified, but they did happen Little One and they are part of your bouquet.

Oh Alma, you are bleeding. I am sorry, let me skate with you and help you. No, Little One, as brave as you are, you cannot stop me bleeding. Don't you realise I only bleed for you? The blood is yours. You are simply looking at my skin of glass and it is like a mirror. I simply bleed for you. Bleeding of the human body can occur internally or externally. The body requires a clot to form to stop the blood flowing. I, Alma, require the clot to be removed. I'm not like any other organ. Human blood empowers me. Distance can't kill me, nor can death. But blood brings life to my inner being. In Isaiah in the Bible: "Jesus poured out his soul through blood into death."

There is power in blood. Can't we unite Little One, can I not come back inside your body? You changed my name to Alma, can I change your name into Spanish? Well, you can't call me Chiquita, that's for my mummy to call me in heaven. But Niña also means Little One, you can use that if you must. That's interesting Niña, if

Snowdrops

we take some letters out of Niña and some out of Alma it spells Maniola – a type of brown meadow butterfly. They can fly when it's dark and most butterflies are inactive then; they are powerful and they spend winter as caterpillars, but when spring arrives, they are so special. They can even fly with damaged wings.

Cannot we enter the cocoon of change together Niña? Yes, Alma I want to be a butterfly, but I worry about all the weeds. Weeds are not hindering you Little One, you just need to change how you manage them. They survive winter by storing food and water in their roots. It's the roots that have the power! You spend too many moments watering these roots. Ruminating over the memories, lift them up from the water. Some weeds can be removed entirely, others remain as a reminder of your growth and some can be used to empathise with other weeds. Don't give the weeds too much power. After all, a weed is simply a plant growing out of place my nana once said. Your weeds need to know their place in your story and with a little thought they can become plants when replanted in the soil of your heart – lift them up out of the water. Lose anything or anyone who feeds your weeds. It is better to be lonely than surrounded by weed feeders: I repeat, lose anything or anyone who feeds your weeds.

Stand up Little One, you are brave, a unique creation, born for purpose, crafted with unique talents and qualities. Look at how snowdrops emerge just as life could not seem bleaker, yet snowdrops pierce the snow-impacted soil with tenacity and vigour. They stand up defiantly against the harsh conditions. Oh, their heads droop a little but they stand none the less, they are pretty, delicate and simplistic flowers to the eye. Yet the tip of the emerging leaf shoot is sharper than a carving knife. Do not be deceived. The snowdrop moves the hearts of the nation. If a snowdrop can withstand winter, do you not feel that you too can stand against all the odds? Oh, your head may droop, Little One, but you can stand in snowdrop moments, even in winter. In fact, the deeper beauty of the snowdrop is often unknown. The bulb is the most valuable part. Unlike the weed that needs its root system contained and stifled, the bulb of the snowdrop splits when dormant and multiplies. Isn't that true of love, kindness and hope when planted in others? It is multiplied too when held. The bulb needs nourishing and nurturing. The bulb is so valuable, yet it has a high cost attached. It's a bit like life; too often people are not prepared to endure the dark woodland walk to see snowdrops carpeting a complete field.

Snowdrops are often found in cemeteries. I like to think that snowdrops appear in cemeteries as the soul of the deceased loved one still has beauty to share with the world, and to act as a reminder to mourners of the snowdrop's hope of reunited hearts and first encounters in heaven.

The snowdrop isn't pollinated, no, the bulb multiplies, deep in the roots. Feed your snowdrop moments deeply, Little One. These plants really are yours. They dance for your birthday; your mummy's

Snowdrops

birthday and they accommodate your chronic hay fever by being non-pollinated plants. Hold them, smell the sweet honey aroma. No antihistamines required; they were made for you. Snowdrops won't be stifled by overcrowding. No, I believe they love to grow in community. Does not love thrive in community? Just as the Spanish dine together as the sun sets on the veranda. The warmth felt is as strong as the sun at midday. Oh, the snowdrop loved and cherished originating in Europe, my heart whispers in Spain. It has to be Spain; I just feel it in my bones. Research has shown that snowdrops help neurological problems like Alzheimer's. I wonder is it because spiritually they reawaken the soul and flood it with memories which evoke all of the five senses. In fact, I wonder does the snowdrop have benefits that the world has yet to discover. Benefits not welcomed due to the limitations set on nature and the divine.

Just watch how the snowdrop seems to eat its warm Weetabix containing its own anti-freeze heating system which melts the surrounding snow. Oh, what if we planted so many snowdrops? Seeds of beauty that the ice age of selfishness and doom melted away. The snowdrop commands the earth, it finds a voice: move I am coming through, nothing will stop me! What about you Little One, do you not have greater means than a snowdrop at your disposal? Of course you do, you just need to stand strong and tell negative forces and obstacles to move and make way for you. After all, this is only a flower, you are so much more than a flower.

Little One's Whisper

Do you know in the backstage of your snowdrop ballet dance on the mountain tops, that the weeds were helping you, by bringing hard-to-get nutrients to the soil's surface feeding your snowdrops? You may know weeds intimately Little One, but you also know the joy of snowdrops kissing you good morning.

You can come home Alma, inside my skin. My home is your home: "Mi casa es su casa." Little One, the composer God will write your fragmented world within. The conductor of your spirit will be the musical equivalent of an inspired force that transmits the message to me Alma. I will amplify your orchestra within and nudge you with equal measures of love and truth. It is your music, orchestra and song just play it from your heart, spirit and soul.

As Little One's symphony of hope starts to begin. Snow, snow, snow, shake, shake, shake. This is the pattern this music can break; snowdrop moments bursting through, weeds taking their place not overcrowding all the grace.

Snow, snow, snow. Shake, shake, shake, spring is getting ready for this glass dome to break, planting seeds of lots of new flowers, ready to bloom in future hours, winter is a season not a life. Now, sing this song Little One with all your might. The violinist and pianist will be by your side when you are too weak to hum, or you're wrestling inside. Do not lose hope, even in your darkest hour, spring is coming my child. The snow is bowing its head to the power of your song sing it often, until winter is gone. This may be your song Little One, but don't forget about every little one that yearns to be free. People in a position of power should fight for this in this land. If they fail to stand up to the quest, then I rest their cases in God's hands praying he overrules man's plan. Jesus can set all children free. PS For you, for us and for them, I write on.

CHAPTER 9

Little Art

Real art is anything that makes something come alive. Art galleries should be closed down. No art gallery is big enough to contain a painter's love, pain or unique journey.

My dad is very artistic, he can draw landscapes and faces. He can capture art in his camera and camcorder. I do not know if my mummy was good at art. No one has ever told me. I guess she is like me as our handwriting is the same somehow. I am artistic to a point, but I get frustrated as my mind is much more creative than my hand allows it to demonstrate. It is a guess though.

Most things I think about my mum are a guess. My grandparents are dead and she was an only child. Everyone else seems too scared to mention her by name. Let alone explore with me her character, or any of her life narrative. I guess she was skilled in art as she could read X-rays at three in the morning and study bones. I wonder did she see beautiful bones, and broken bones. Not just fractures, but broken bones in the spiritual realm. I see art when I look at photos of her, particularly her eyes. They were like the sea. Sometimes a mint green, other times a more definite blue. Oh, her life was art. As I lift my pen on Mother's Day weekend, I draw in memory of her. Her art is my art. It lives in my blood. Fifty per cent of me is her, I may not look exactly like her apart from my eyes. My dad and I have physical similarities. Yet at moments of peace, I see her in the mirror.

Birth Mummy, I miss whatever could have been. You will never see me grow up, you will be forever missing at every significant milestone of my life. People don't understand the depth of that loss, but I wish skin was glass as they would see the mummy-shaped void in my heart. I have planted flowers in there. Blue hydrangeas, just for you. Can I draw for you Birth Mummy, can I tell you what's wrong? Alma will help me; she lives inside me now. I can call for her and she comes out to play. I smooth the snow with my stick to make my very own canvas on the ground. I close my eyes and allow my brush to move. I feel uncertain. After all, I can't draw like dad. So, does that mean I cannot access the art within? Every child I know loves drawing. The problem is to remain an artist when we grow up. So, I have to reverse what I have been taught, I have to trust the brush in my hand, and start again.

You see, life is art. Everyone has art in them; it expresses it itself in unique ways. The way Annie made sandwiches was art. The lighting of a perfectly balanced log fire is art. Making a high grade cappuccino is art. The French seem to excel in this. Handwriting is art, as is putting flowers – even wild flowers – in an old wine bottle after a spring walk. However, grown-ups have taken artistic expression and categorised it into fine art, modern art and sculptures to name but a few. If your unique artistic expression does not fall neatly into a category your art is rendered inadequate. My favourite artwork is that of a three-year-old little one. It doesn't follow rules or symmetry and often pushes past the boundaries of the black lines. I wonder how many people could access healing if we lifted the artistic expression of the soul.

Real art is anything that makes something come alive. Art galleries should be closed down. No art gallery is big enough to contain a painter's love, pain, or unique journey. As Antony Gormley's iron men have become public art, it is subjected to graffiti, vandalism, flash photography and admiration. Community deepens art's value. I think Antony knew that and put the Angel of the North on display to comfort the sad commuter to the motorway of despair, illness and depression. The erosion of the elements further deepens Antony's work as the waves take their pain out on these iron statues. All art should be public and accessible to all. I don't care any more if I have been told I am not artistic; I want my picture suspended in the sky from the clouds with brass hooks. I want other people to stop, see their pain in it. To see inspiration in it, to move in it and respond by loving harder, loving longer and loving wider. Man is made in the image of God with a unique Alma.

God is the best artist in the world. Look at the stars in the sky, and the moonlight casting a purple haze. Look at the sky with the sun rising majestically and going to sleep in colours of blazing red. Oh, the world is art. We are art, and paintbrushes long to be lifted from the dusty shelves of the soul as they say let me stroke it better. Let me deepen the tone, enhance the light and re-awaken emotion. In fact, art in its broader sense longs for the crushed dancer to move again. For the forgotten singer to find a new song. Art tugs at the chords of the musician saying let me play once more. Art is liberating and pulls us into a deeper connection to the Alma in true individualism and originality.

The teacher who told me I could not draw as well as my sister, missed my art. She missed my attempt at saying I am hurting; I have a monster in my house. Think carefully before discriminating in art, every picture is trying to tell a story. I nervously lift my paintbrush and dip the dry bristles into a cup of water. My canvas is smooth, so I begin to draw the outline of a little winter tree. The dark black paint outline stands out in contrast to the snow. Oh, this tree does know moments of being dressed in vibrant green, smelling like freshly pressed laundry and familiar to the sound of birds taking shelter away from the blazing sunshine. Oh, this tree has worn a wardrobe of autumnal depth and enjoyed the company of crisp leaves. This tree has also enjoyed the sound of the whispering trees of spring, laced in leaves and budding shoots as carolling birds play in delight.

Yet these branches also know what it is like to endure winter. The tree is now bare and casts dark shadows on the snow as the sun sits lower in the winter sky. Its bark is as wrinkled as my very own palms on my hands. The winter tree suffers the harsh elements in silence. People paint winter trees and use them on Christmas cards and marvel at their beauty. However, they ignore how sparse the tree is and how barren and broken. I think

Little Art

winter trees cry and their pain is strong enough to pass this emotion to the next generation in the forest. You see, trees thrive in community. In my drawing my tree stands alone. My tree is in fact me, Little Tree, Little One, the mother tree shades and protects. Yet the absence of this mother tree and the environment I dwell in, leaves me living through winter moments alone and in silence.

Sometimes I try to speak, but mostly I react badly to people I feel are trying to hurt me. Because of this, Hands and my dad take me to see the doctor. They think my poor behaviour is a disease. I twist my hair all the time and it snaps off like an icy winter branch. Do they not see, no child reacts badly in most cases, unless they are trying to communicate pain through undeveloped resources? My paintbrush moves more quickly now and the forms and shapes are showing twirling, twisting branches. Some pointing vertically others horizontally, but mainly these branches are upwards and diagonal. Some twigs are hanging onto the tree for their lives, so thin and fragile they are at risk of snapping in this frost, and from the weight of the snow.

Some branches are strong and show the maturity of a tree over 200 years in age. These branches communicate across the atmosphere come on snow fall on me I am not scared of your flakes. My strong branches have been nourished by Annie love, Nana Riah, Grandad. The secure, happy moments in high summer skimming stones with my dad. Time spent on the numerous farms on my paternal side. Swinging from trees on an old tractor tyre, fishing and swimming in the river. Feeding the lambs and climbing haystacks and making dens. Coming in and having treats from the Aga cooker and running up the path to collect the bread from the bread van and receiving a lollipop. Endless nights with my cousins playing and preparing midnight feasts. My strong branches are also a testimony of the love that pours into my trunk from special teachers, friends and other significant people. What an art to breathe life into my picture: to positively impact the life of a little one is sacred art. I may be little, but I know love, my branches thrive. My picture almost magnifies, my tree enlarges. People so often are good at making things look picture perfect! Yet I was happier having no mummy than having a family portrait that looked serene yet contained hidden shadows!

Think about the suffering of silence felt by little ones the world over, by distorting their drawing too quickly, too carelessly and too much. I also know what breaks and crushes my branches; I know what makes them curl into the foetus position. I am scared of Hands, I am scared of her control, her screaming, her violent outbursts. The times that she grabs me by the hair and screams in my face with so much hatred that her spittle lands on my face. I'm scared when she hits my sister and leaves my dad. I am scared when she has gone away as I know it is not forever. She packs her suitcase and leaves for her parents' house. Or she goes on long drives in her car until my dad's frantic with worry over her safety. This is very manipulative behaviour.

Little Art

My dad talks to me about it on days away. Yet on those day trips my stomach churns; I know in time he will surrender once again to her return. She controls everything and everyone – the house, my appearance – she does not touch my play, probably because she is glad to get rid of me. Yet I get anxious playing football as, if I am five minutes late home, she will go mad. I hate her. I am starting to scream back, barricade myself and push her back. I hate myself. I hate hurting anyone, even a spider on the ground. My branches shake in fear and anger simultaneously.

I am not going to the farms as much. You see, Hands had a fight with two of my aunts. She is insecure and does not like them chatting to my dad showing pictures of my mum. My dad over-reacts and I get in the car as he speeds off. Nothing is ever sorted calmly; my branches shake, my heart breaks, I do not know the finer details, but I know it is wrong. These women looked after me as a baby. I belong with them. The summers in Northern Ireland are eight weeks long. I now spend at least four of them with Hands' mum in the city. I don't want to be in the city. This woman does not want me around – she never shouts, or hits me, she does not even tell me off, but I know it is a chore for her. So, I go out most of the time and call on friends.

My church pastor lives around the corner and they have a big play area. I am always welcome, I play with his children, my sister and the other little ones. We fill paddling pools and play tennis, we get up to lots of innocent mischief too. I'm happy on the streets, the milkman even lets us ride on the back of his float. I am free outside and at all my clubs – people wonder why my skin is so brown. I am out most of the day, Hands comes back at 2pm every day in the summer, but I try not to come home until five when tea is ready, or I invite friends over. You see I get friends to come to tea and stay as Hands controls herself then. If the weather is nice, I put up the five-man tent in the garden. Yet on nights alone the shadow of my tree scares me. The shadow of Hands in my mind scares me. Don't you see, little ones are like trees; they suffer in the woods alone. Ellas sufren solo en el bosque.

CHAPTER 10

Shifting Shadows

Snow, snow, snow. Shake, shake, shake. Spring is getting ready for this glass dome to break. Planting seeds of lots of new flowers. Ready to bloom in future hours.

Alma, help me! Can you feel it Alma, can you feel my pain? The flashbacks to my branches being shaken are real. I can be hard at play one minute and a smell, or a place, can bring these memories flooding through my mind. Look at my canvas on the snow Alma. A bare tree holding on for the hope of spring. The canvas painting is hung upside down as my snow globe tremors.

I can't see a way to fix this picture Alma; it's ruined. I am ruined, spoilt and damaged goods. Isn't that what people say? I hear them, Alma, labelling people and at times even writing them off. Voicing well-meant judgements and opinions. My picture is real, Alma. Does anyone really want to hold and cherish an upside-down winter tree, when they can hold beautiful autumn, summer and spring ones? Should I not just accept defeat and accept the cards that life has dealt me? I hear and feel the rejection of Hands grow louder and louder. You see she hurt me in an already broken place. To lose my mum was one thing; to have someone step in and cause pain in that broken place is almost too much for me to carry.

She really hurt me. She continues to hurt me. She even told me if my Birth Mummy was alive that she would hate me. I know this is a lie but like most little ones, I believe the lies of grown-ups. The fact that they are grown-ups makes you powerless to contest the lies at times. Hands used my wound to empower her own interest in asserting dominance. I am worthless, Alma, I am a freak, an unlovable freak. Oh, don't get me wrong, in many ways I'm still strong. I still feel all other seasons of tree life. It's just when pain hits me afresh, my strength and courage drop like leaves of a tree leaving me bare and naked, reaching out for secure foundation. It is like I'm spinning on black ice at times. Strong but weak. Wise but searching for solutions. Oh Alma, I want to suspend my picture without fear, but the reality is, I am scared. Scared of the magnified shadow over my life, scared no one can help me not even you; my fear tempts me into silence.

Oh, Little One, my Niña, it is OK to be scared. Your will is strong, you know what you want to achieve but that does not come without a cost. Not everyone can help, not even I. I am your soul but you need more than soul to navigate your snow dome conditions, Little One. You need me, Alma, to connect to God. That connection to the Trinity of the Father, Son and Holy Spirit will feed your soul. You then need to surrender to Sofia. Sofia ... what is Sofia, Alma? Sofia is not really a person, Little One, it simply means the wisdom of God. Why do I need the wisdom of God, Alma? I mean, do I really need more help? Yes, Little One, everyone needs Sofia to engage in their past, present and future moments.

Little One's Whisper

I have never met Sofia before, how can I get to know Sofia? Psalm 119 makes that clear, Little One. The respectful fear of God is the beginning of wisdom. James 15:8 goes on to say if any of you lacks wisdom ask for it and it will be given to you. Alma, I understand my pain, why do I need wisdom when I have understanding? It's because it's more than natural knowledge, humility births wisdom. James 3:17 "The wisdom that comes from heaven is first of all pure, then peace-bringing, considerate, submissive, full of mercy and good fruit."

Earthly wisdom appeals to the senses and emotions. In contrast, the wisdom that is from God reflects him. Don't be fooled Little One by people in positions of power and worldly riches. They may be successful, but not all success is wise. Oh, earthly wisdom tells us to follow our hearts, look after number one, while Jeremiah 17:9 reminds us that the heart is deceitful above all things. Earthly wisdom says seeing is believing ... whereas in John 20:29 it states; "Blessed are those who have not seen and yet have believed." Earthly wisdom says there are many ways to God. Yet Godly wisdom tells us in Acts 4:12 "There is only one way to God through Jesus." In fact, the longest chapter in the Bible is Psalm 119 and it is all about gaining wisdom.

Alma moves in everyone Little One. You can have soul music without knowing God. Yet the most alive soul is one who knows God and invites Sofia into their lives. You know you have heard from Sofia when words of life are spoken, when hope reawakens and when peace floods in like the ocean. So many people walk close to the edge of the exposed sand allowing their toes to be dipped in water. Yet very few embrace Sofia fully. Oh, they may on a Sunday morning, or on Christmas Eve midnight mass. Yet without allowing Sofia to encompass every memory and thought, every feeling. Then at some point the tide will reside. Oh God will still be there, waiting for surrender. To walk in the wisdom of God, to hold Sofia's hand requires more than faith.

You know this to be, Little One, I watch you dip your toes in and out. Won't you swim in the depths of Sofia carried by the arms of God? It requires an act of submission, yet don't you see in that submission is the power to smash your snow dome? Humility is more powerful than pride. Oh Alma … you make it sound so easy. I am not sure Sofia can help me. Well, Little One, let me tell you a story, a long time ago lived a man named George Matterson, he was in love and awaiting to be married but was turning blind – his fiancé refused to marry him upon hearing the news. I think he surrendered his pain to Sofia one lonely night in Scotland when he penned the hymn, *Oh Love That Wilt Not Let Me Go*. I feel he did not try to fix this mess, despite being intelligent enough to teach Queen Victoria. I wonder if he knew that only Sofia could speak into his dark picture, into his grief and loss. Listen, Little One, listen to the words in the song, "Oh love that will not let me go."

I ponder did George Matheson allow God to shift his

shadows? Did Sofia become his best friend and closest confident? Little One, shadows are not that scary. Shadows form over many aspects of our lives. They lurk around appearing disproportionate in size and form. They are dark, they pretend to be real, but they can only form when they project themselves on the opposite surface of a source of light.

Shadows can shift if the object moves, you can't change what happened, earthly wisdom would focus on trying to move the object through mindfulness or online distraction. The wisdom of God whispers you can also move a shadow by lifting the sun in the sky. The sun here refers to the solar sun, but I mean lift the Son of God higher, above your picture. He can shift shadows through healing. Shadows are shortest around noon when the position of the sun is highest in the sky.

Earthly wisdom blames God for shadows. Yet interestingly, the time when the sun is at its most powerful is the same time that Jesus was crucified. God not only moved shadows he removed the light completely and covered the earth in darkness. His pain perhaps was too deep for shadows, it demanded a solar eclipse when people blame God for suffering. They fail to see his grief, not just in the shadows of the cross shown on Jesus' own winter tree, but a grief so deep it required the sun to close off every ray. No shadows, no light. Little One, God shifted shadows on the cross in dramatic darkness as the earth quaked.

I wonder did heaven become a snow globe on the

Shifting Shadows

day of Jesus' crucifixion. God could no longer be in intimate communication with Jesus due to Jesus taking on himself humanity's sin. The Bible makes this clear as it states Jesus cried out, "My God, my God, why have you forsaken me?" Matthew 27:46. I believe it was even more painful for God to not have intimacy with his son as heaven was sealed in a sphere of snow globe separation. Of course, this is not biblical fact but I see it in my mind's eye none the less.

Can you imagine God in heaven playing a moving picture frame sat upon his icy shelf? Can you imagine it flipping through images of Jesus throughout his life, his miraculous birth, his ministry on Earth and tender moments with Joseph and Mary around the supper table? The shadow of the cross being seen over every image. The images are piercing yet I believe the shadows of humanity's sin moved him more. God had no choice but to silently watch as his only son was lacerated, and nails were pierced into his hands. In fact, this is incorrect, he did have a choice. Twelve thousand legions could have delivered Jesus with a click of God's finger, yet I maintain he had no real choice. His love for us overpowered any rescue plan. The crucifixion of his beloved son had to occur to allow us the opportunity for an intimate romance with God. To receive his unconditional and passionate love, the overwhelming all-consuming thirst for God to be your everything.

Over the years, humanity has tried to add conditions to this love. Nothing we do can earn it. Nothing we do could stop it. It is simply a free gift. God wants us to be free. Some people think religion is all about rules and stifling freedom, I don't know what is stifling about his love. God longs to hold you, to heal you, to whisper tenderly into the bruised and broken places in your soul. God simply wants you and me in his arms, locked in an intimate dance, in the fullness of life. The world needs to get back to the basics of this love affair. Do not hide behind religion. Focus on the passion that God has for you. The passion he showed on the cross. This is the only religious title you need.

As Jesus took on our sin, he was for the first time unable to address God as his father. I wonder was there a snowstorm in heaven momentarily. Oh, the loss of this divine attachment broken for you, for us and for them. I wonder did heaven freeze over so deeply that the Antarctic felt tropical. Jesus himself I believe was encased in his own snow globe on the cross. His mother, Mary, wept at the foot of the cross but no touch could be shared between them. No touch could be shared with his father. Yet the untouched saviour of the world still took the time to touch the heart of the thief encased in the snow globe with him at Calvary. This man, unworthy of love and forgiveness, was loved and forgiven.

Some people blame God for suffering, yet both God and Jesus suffered so much. We live in a broken world, we will suffer in it. There will be disease and tragedy. Yet because of the suffering of Jesus and God we can journey through this painful life with their first-hand experience in pain. They, I believe, are moved deeply by our sorrow and the only thing that stops this intimate rescue is sin. Humanity's snow globe was smashed at the cross. If only people would freely receive the love that overpowers snow globe entrapment.

Allow him to reframe it for you. I believe he wants to fulfil your dreams to suspend your picture on brass hooks in the sky. Not to be viewed in shame, but to be a reminder that most pictures are only fragments of the big picture; that shadows are longer in winter, but no shadow has to be permanent. If you can't move the object move the sun. Ask God to give you the vision that can see beyond the picture and through the picture … trusting that the golden shadows of God will overpower the most traumatic winter night in your mind. Try Little One, try to trust and remember Little One; "Every good and perfect gift is from above, coming down from the father of heavenly lights, who does not change like shifting shadows," James 1:17.

Humans can only help to a degree. Shadows can always emerge afresh, but God is a constant in the chaos. Sofia, will you try for you, for us, for them? Well, Little One, what do you think? I am scared. You see I know in my heart that this is all true, yet I feel disloyal. I feel tempted to focus on the many times that things were OK; I had parties and lots of play. Hands loved me sometimes. My dad tried his best, my mind wants to suppress my weak-branch experiences in favour of all the nice meals out. The times where normality reigned, the spring and summer memories. Yet my story is also full of my autumn and winter pain. The pain that eats like a cancer. Without apology inside the shame, the guilt of even remembering – yet alone validating it – is overwhelming.

I think of those with more pain more intense than mine; I try to reduce my experience. I am tempted to tilt my canvas to hide the bad bits, but my arms have grown weak over the years. I can't hold it in that angle any more. I surrender, if only in part, I look up as God, Jesus and the Holy Spirit lead on by their kindly light. I surrender more: I need help, I need healing, I need to cry; I need to say it hurts, it hurts. It hurts to try to protect everyone from my bad memories. It hurts to feel disloyal even committing this pain to paper. It hurts physically. It is like my body grieves and my mouth aches as it releases every vowel and consonant as I speak the words of these pages aloud.

The alphabet spirals around my mind, remembering Hands' family who seemed aloof. It spins recalling times of such fear, rejection, dismissal and suppression. It wasn't normal. It is not normal to be scared in your own home. Sofia, at times I don't know if I hate Hands, or I hate myself for not finding a way to escape. I am not sure why my dad couldn't see in my eyes the pain I didn't speak, I ached.

I ache, Sofia, I won't lie – the prospect of embracing you isn't appealing. You require my all, and I was happy it being just Alma and me. I am afraid of being close to people and you want my every breath. I mean you are not even real. How do I know I can trust your guidance with my story? I close my eyes. I want to hide from you.

Yet as my eyes rest in darkness I see you, I really see you my imaginary friend. You leave through the door of a blue cottage on a hill and you are whispering in tune and rhyme my very own song: "Snow, snow, snow. Shake, shake, shake." This is the pattern this music can break, snowdrop moments bursting through, weeds standing in their place not overcrowding all the grace.

Snow, snow, snow, shake, shake, shake. Spring is getting ready for this glass dome to break, planting seeds of lots of new flowers ready to bloom in future hours. Winter is a season, not a life, now sing this song loud Little One, with all of your might! The snow is bowing its head at the power of your song, sing it loud until winter is gone.

Sofia sings and dances dressed in white holding wild flowers; she is pure, has curly blonde hair and a delicate nose. I reach out, holding Alma with one hand stretched out and reach out tentatively with my other hand to touch my imaginary friend. She spins in delight looking like a white butterfly. I see flashes of her tiptoeing, spinning and sprinting into the circumstances of others, oh, like me, so many reject Sofia, after all, you have to see beyond seeing to view her. Yet, I wonder can they smell her. She smells like an April shower in Spain as it evokes the aroma of citrus and honeysuckle. I look down and notice Sofia has old and wrinkled feet. I wonder if this is because she never stops wandering barefooted for people who are searching for her in all the wrong places. I repeat, she never stops wandering barefooted for people who are searching for her in all the wrong places. She does not live in libraries, universities or in government. She lives in nature and she is not frightened to knock on the doors where people are hiding depths of pain. She whispers in my ear, wisdom requires sacrifice and suffering yet in wisdom there is peace, a profound paradox.

I open my eyes and prepare to divide my afternoon tea by three, there will be a cost in my choice to embrace Sofia. It will cost more than my clotted-cream scones and my cucumber sandwiches. It will cost more than my tea served in floral china teacups. It will cost more than the most decadent chocolate brownie. Yet to feel and see her, and continue to reject her, I would be forever living in the shadows of my destiny. Before I welcome Sofia to join me, I must get to work on designing some sandals. No little one likes old and smelly feet.

For you, for us, for them, I have surrendered all of my canvas – it is now no longer my hidden art, it is exposed and revealed, I see God has placed it in the sky. I have no idea how this surrendered picture will influence the final piece. But there is a lightness in lifting the sun, the shadows are shifting, as I have raised the sun over my circumstance the snowflakes of God's tears are beginning to cover this canvas scene in new beginnings of cleansing and healing. P.S. Winter is only a season. El invierno es solo una temporada.

CHAPTER 11

Icy Surrender

If you do not surrender to God, you will surrender to something.

Alma, Sofia, are you there? I cannot hear you, or see you, or smell you both? I know you are there, but my senses are all consumed with anger, hurt and pain. I have come so far on my snow globe journey and collapsed in a heap to look up and see a snowy covered mountain. I won't carry on! You must help me! I mean it, speak and protest to God on my behalf. This has to stop! I want out! Smash my glass dome! Is it too much to ask? I mean I simply want a home. That is not an excessively unreasonable request. I hate this life! It is hurting me; it is stopping me in my tracks. It's stripping me of everything I know. If this is how you help people it is not nice, cruel in fact. Leave me! After all, you cannot even be bothered to speak to me, or caress me in my pain.

I want new friends. Friends that care, and bring joy wrapped in a box with a big red bow. I want to laugh until I feel my sides will split. Your companionship is disappointing beyond belief! I thought we could bake cakes together, light a fire and boil the kettle for tea in a china cup. I wanted to tell you about my interior design for my new home, but I am not telling you now. This kingdom I'm dreaming of will never appear. It is an illusion; a mirage I have been tricked into believing my

Icy Surrender

life could be anything more than snow globe encased. Now it is a snow globe, that is shaken violently in my pursuit of spring.

How dare you give me false hope! How can you arouse feelings of new beginnings and brighter tomorrows but not bring that to fruition? You do not even really know me. I mean, I am really creative, I can make this kingdom creation on my very own. I see each room in my little one kingdom. I can hear the fire crackling over Irish turf, and I smell the aroma of fresh fig, mandarin and basil candles enveloping the hallway. I can even taste the freshly baked tea bread, finished with a lavish spreading of real butter, served on a butterfly and blue hydrangea patterned plate. I am so tired of this journey; my life is unrecognisable.

As I have journeyed through the past ten chapters, I have expected to see a faint glimmer of the lights from my new kingdom fit for a princess shining in the distance. Instead I see a mountain covered in snow, which blocks my vision to the rest of the landscape across my path. How do you expect me to carry on? It has already been a long journey. I do not have the strength to climb mountains! This is so frustrating, unsettling and unnerving. I can see from my peripheral view, friends enjoying hot chocolate with marshmallows and whipped cream. I do not like whipped cream or hot chocolate, but I'd like some marshmallows. I would like a break from the rigorous journey to luxuriate in marshmallow eating. I'd toast them and dip them in the hot chocolate to melt them whilst listening to uplifting Yuletide songs and enhancing my life with new friendships and connections, and dancing with current loved ones. But no, I cannot even do that, I am listening to *In the Bleak Midwinter* on repeat.

The pain I feel is similar to that of a toothache: when the body is in pain it swells. The swelling is simply from the movement of fluid and white blood cells rushing to the source of pain to comfort – like a mother rushes to her knee-grazed child. This swelling also prevents further injury, but teeth don't swell they are solid. When they hurt, they throb and nothing except a visit to the dentist can even lessen the pain. That's how my pain feels in this snow globe, like toothache. It can't swell as it's gagged inside this snow dome! It throbs, silently throbs. Sometimes the external shaking of my world makes it feel like multiple tooth pain bouncing around like the pinballs released by the trigger from a hyperactive child at the fairground. So, what have you both got to say for yourselves? Judgement perhaps, condemning me for being human, for lacking faith at this time, for even distrusting the hand of God.

Go on, judge me! At least I am honest and brave enough to tell you the truth. It hurts the truth, doesn't it? It hurts to be told that your well-meant offerings are insufficient. Well, it's out there now and I'm going to sit here watching people build snowmen, having fun, enjoying life. Oh, I know they may be hiding their wounds under duffle coats and winter hats, but perhaps that's better than being stripped bare to the door of pain, alone and cold. I am having a rest ... show up, or

Icy Surrender

don't. I do not care! I can catch a cable car to the top of the mountain. I can jump in the car of people going on ski holidays. I am 12 now, my hands are bigger. I may even be able to break this glass myself. I could forget this journey altogether and decorate an igloo. I know it could be OK, after all, I have free will. This is my life. My decision, my time to escape! I've had enough of the pain. It hurts physically, emotionally and spiritually. I awake in the morning and open my eyes to fresh snow. The weather won't change. The season is stuck like an old record on repeat.

Shake, shake, shake, snow, snow, snow, this is all I seem to know. Maybe that is a little negative, I must confess – there are bursts of sunshine that come through from time to time to give me rest. But I can't own them or claim them to melt this cold harsh land… they slip through my fingers like fine grains of sand! Running from me like a refugee to a foreign land.

I look for bright moments every day, I try and help myself come what may. Yet this climate is heavy. It weighs a ton and quite simply my strength is almost done. When I am blessed with words, a friend that seems to understand, I find shelter from this winter test, but if the truth be told my soul is full of unrest. I try to pray, I cry out to God, I do not want any more time to pass. My knees are sore from praying for release, but heaven doesn't send down the key to unlock the door and set me free. I do not like getting cross and sad, but this cabin fever is driving me mad. Please can I just get out fast, as I am tempted to destroy this glass. I know it's not going to bring lasting peace – if I take this into my own hands it's not really the perfect plan.

Yet I am not sure if I have the strength to last this test of time and I try to look at things from a different view, but I simply can't make daisy chains from snow, can you? The conditions are out of my control. I repeat, I've no control of my conditions. This is what scares me the most, no matter how hard I try. I can't devise a plan to get out as I know without God's approval from above that spring may not appear. But my life will lack the full impact of this love somehow, I must be true to this call. If I can truly know peace above it all. Sitting alone, my mind drifts off into a daydream to find a temporary escape. Alma, Sofia, I didn't mean to be so mean. Can you please show yourselves again to me? Time ticks by, tick-tock, tick-tock, all I do is watch the invisible clock.

The night grows darker, it has gone black. But when I look up to the stars in the sky, I see them shining and dancing way up high. They bring me a moment of joy, wonder and awe. These amazing shapes in the sky remind me that I am in the hands of such an amazing creator called God, if he hung the stars in all their splendour tonight, can he help me again in my ongoing fight? As if by a click of his finger I see butterflies flying quickly towards me, the Holy Spirit drawing close. They kiss me so tenderly and whisper: we care. God sent them to me to let me know he hasn't forgotten me out in the snow. Off they fly to visit someone else, but one waits beside me, it won't leave me until I get strong,

Icy Surrender

it stays close by singing my song. Even when I get strong, I think it rests on my chest, after, all it says in the Bible his love never rests. He will never leave me, or forsake me at all. Yet at times I confess I forget this promise, I really do. Don't we all at times, don't you?

*

The black ice lies underneath unseen by the naked eye, even by the endless passers-by. I am grateful for the fun snow days and the times Daddy and Hands enjoy my sister and I. Still, I would rather erase the snow from my life. I am tired from shouting inside my dome. So, I settle into bed to watch TV. Oh, *The Snowman* is playing on every channel, its iconic theme booming inside my snow globe – *Walking in the Air*. Oh, it is lonely here in bed, so I welcome the snowman as my friend. I have popcorn and Coca-Cola in a glass bottle. Oh, what naughty snacks when I have already brushed my teeth. I don't really care; I need a snow day off from this life. Yet, snow is simply snow, no matter how you dress it up. It is so icy, such cold, cold stuff.

The morning arrives, the dawn breaks, Alma and Sofia are there by my side. The butterfly was my physician and comforter during the night, and when I let go of the hatred and rage my vision was restored, my friends in plain sight. Ready for battle between good and evil. Eager to help me once again to undress the anger which covered the pain. No matter how much I protest, their love remains consistent and fair. I like

Little One's Whisper

that. Alma, Sofia, it's so good to see you both. Good morning, have we got time for coffee? They smile, we gather round the icy café. I am stuck, look at this mountain. How can I get out? I'm exhausted and need help.

Oh, Little One we would like you to join us in a prayer. Not the demanding angry ones, even though God listens to those, too, but we instead encourage you to say aloud the words that your nana taught you by the open fire before bed. OK, I will say it, but I pray to God in Spanish, so I'm saying it in Spanish. That is OK, Little One. It is known to God in every language but not said enough, and yet people wonder why the world is in such a mess when Jesus taught us what to say.

"Our Father, who art in heaven, hallowed be thy name: thy kingdom come... Padre nuestro que estas en los cielos santificado sea tu ombre venga tu reino..."

I need to stop. I cannot carry on. Little One, you are searching for your kingdom. Yet you are not surrendering to the divine will of God in totality, we urge you to surrender and bow to the sovereignty of God over your life. But I've listened and written ten chapters in an attempt to surrender my pain is that not enough? Little One, that was pleasing that you did that. Yet, you are so busy looking for an escape that you do not seem to see that those ten chapters are on your back, you drag them everywhere holding on the words and pages for comfort. They are weighing you down and need to be relinquished if you aim to journey on.

You see, Little One, listen a minute. You sometimes

Icy Surrender

listen to Alma (the soul) and to Sofia (the wisdom of God) and God. Yet, do you welcome the Holy Spirit to help you discern and guide you? You are scared to submit because you think by being vulnerable you are open to attack. Jesus himself lived a life of submission to the will of his father. There is freedom in surrendering to God. It does not matter what people taught you about submission to authority, they abused that teaching. It is a teaching mutilated the world over, that follows the idea if you pursue biblical truths it will lead to a dull life. This could not be further from the truth – let's look to the example of Jesus. "Whoever wants to be my disciple must deny themselves and take up their cross and follow me," Matthew 16:24.

I do not believe the cross is not symbolic of a burden. No, it is symbolic of death. Dying to self, so that your body is God's property. How can you follow God's path with chapters on your back, which weigh you down? Can you surrender them over to God and take up your cross instead? You carry them on your back bursting from a brown leather double-buckle satchel. The one you had on your first day of school. The leather is damaging your back. It causes friction with each new step on your journey.

Surrender then? Do you know what you are asking of me? Yes, Little One, we know. Yet we ask again, will you let go, even lose them on purpose? After all, how can you one day live complete in a kingdom without full surrender to the king. You can surrender to God's adoption of you, to his provision of a father, a very daughter of the king. His kingdom is one of love, joy, peace, patience, kindness, goodness and self-control. Safety is not found in your ten chapters, it is found in him. I struggle to surrender, to submit it scares me. What if I get abused again and taken advantage of? Little One, life offers no guarantees. Yet if you do not surrender to God, you will still surrender to something. I repeat, if you do not surrender to God, you will still surrender to something. That may be greed, or a life full of misery, it is only he who truly loses his life that will find it. I know, but do you realise that I am being asked to surrender the pain of losing my mother, the loss of my grandparents, the fight for my soul, my snowdrop moments and skin? I am being asked to let go of my art, my shadows, my dance on the ice. My book to date, my life on pages?

Little One, these chapters form your life, by surrendering them you are not forgetting them, you can still learn from them, and reflect on them. But they cannot consume you. The good moments and the bad. They are in the past and can be viewed in a historical sense, yet you are hauling them around in your present journey and wondering why you are growing weary. You are waiting for a mother who will never return, those teenage fights won't happen, she can't help you on your wedding day. No, she is gone. Lost, a loss you need to fully embrace. She's gone, but you won't let her go. Your mother's chapter is the primary chapter, which you cling to like glue, frightened that loss, hurt and pain could arise again.

Icy Surrender

Some chapters, like Annie love, comfort you and you cling to those for security in hard times. These memories will always be yours, but they can bring you freedom from the fear of loss and betrayal. You may never have a love as strong as Annie love again, but you can use that chapter to bring Annie love to others. How can I surrender? Simply ask God to heal all the broken pieces in all the last ten chapters. Thank him for the blessings too, then simply let go. OK, I will try. One by one, I surrender:

Oh, look Alma, Sofia, I am standing on the top of the mountain. Yes, God's strength carried you there. The icy fell of surrender. The only scene that is visible in my snow globe landscape, is the very top of the mountain. No matter how much the snow falls, this scene is unmovable. I rub my eyes. I try to change the picture in my mind. It is still there. I close them. I slam my eyelids shut. Then slowly begin to open them… section by section, the same vision appears.

There, waits a bobsleigh. It awaits occupation and descent. God knows you are tired and has provided a bobsleigh for our descent down the far side of the fell. It will be bumpy; it will be like stepping into the unknown with every twist and turn unrevealed until it presents itself, yet take comfort, Little One, you are not alone. We are in it together, quite literally encased in our bobsleigh as one. This is the scariest choice I have ever made; I am already broken and fragile and don't like heights. What if I get hurt? What if it hurts more not to try?

Little One's Whisper

OK, I will bobsleigh. Before we jump inside the bobsleigh I hope I have a helmet as I'm scared. I am equally scared to know that I can't escape you three in this close proximity, and frightened of the unknown path ahead. This is an extreme sport and I am so little, I am only 12 coming on 13. Yet I trust that by letting go, I'm travelling towards freedom. I look back momentarily, to flashes of fun in winter, at the Continental markets, their wooden huts ablaze with tempting produce. I simply bow my head, I close my eyes and surrender. Let the descent from the icy fell of surrender commence after one, two, three.

CHAPTER 12

The Bobsleigh Track

*Who knows how big the human heart can grow?
How much can skin stretch when it is healed
from pain?*

Encased, surrounded and curled tightly in my rickety bobsleigh. My bobsleigh is not like the ones you see displayed at the Winter Olympics. No, mine is gunmetal, unpainted, unpolished and raw. A rickety old bobsleigh for me. It is so old; it looks so unpolished. It looks slightly unsafe if I am honest. It squeaks as though I am not the first little one who has ever crept inside. That brings me a strange sense of comfort, a knowledge that I am not the first, nor may I be the last to make this emotional and knuckle-whitening ride.

Bobsleighing is not for the weak, the faint-hearted and frail. It is an extreme sporting event, many people engaging in this have even crashed to their death. It requires you to isolate yourself from others, to be prepared to follow an unknown track, it demands commitment to the end, as there are no pit stops or U-turns on the course. It fills me with fear, if the truth be told, as my bobsleigh journey defies my natural desire to carefully follow a safe-cut plan. It means I must follow this track not by sight, but simply by faith, will God keep me safe, will he hold my hand, will he bring relief? What if I get hurt? This is what spins around in my head, yet my heart knows this is the next step in my quest to unburden myself; to ease this unrest.

The moment is here, the time has arrived, and I have bowed my head and lowered my pride. This is unnatural, it seems so unfair as I want to be in control of how I share my pain. But the path is set out it has been ready for some time, my only request I must protest is that I need one toy to comfort my path. Perhaps my own angel, albeit it pocket sized. I know as I sit awaiting my descent that my time of physical comfort from Alma and Sofia cannot remain. They need to be inside me now, so that I can hold onto God with my two tiny hands. To have nothing in the way – holding to him tightly. This is not something I could have done before this time you see. I did not know I would put my trust in God to this degree, nor did I know that he was prepared to journey with me so intimately. Yet I feel him so close, I hear him say, "In your pain, I will always stay."

Alma and Sofia will always now be a part of the inside of me, they will speak to me often especially when I'm alone. They will warn me of danger and remind me not to follow man's plan as the soul and wisdom of God; Alma and Sofia named them as you know They will be used by God to communicate in some ways. Yet I need to now experience his full, undiluted power. A moment with my father in the sky, a connection is awaiting like never before. It goes beyond salvation, religion or prayers. It is simply acknowledging him as my father and my God who cares. Yet

God knows me more than most. He knows that I sometimes need a tangible sign ... after all, I am a visual learner and creative at heart. He knows I need a little comfort on my way. As Alma and Sofia move house, from the snow globe into my heart, an angel as tiny as can be breaks from her own little ball of glass. After all, it says in the Bible, we all have our own angel every day when we believe in Christ and bow the knee. He sets that little angel free.

The only people now on the physical journey, from here to the end, will be God my father, me Little One and my angel friend. I will name her Angelito just as she is Spanish for 'little angel' summed up in one word. It sounds so gentle, yet it also too sounds strong even though she is made of glass. She will survive. Even if she has to lose one of her delicate wings. I know that she will stay by my side, squashed in my pocket as it is very cold outside.

Before this journey begins, I need to say this out loud: this journey seems cruel and I am tempted to shrink away even though I am getting so big and strong. I do not want to hurt my adult body any more. It is never anything I have stopped long enough to consider, yet her life for the last two years has been very cold and bitter. It is not my place to state all the things that have gone on. Yet it is like the more I grow the more I heal, the more room I am taking up of her body, mind and soul. That is something that may bring delight in the end. Yet in this transition I am neither there nor is she, as she was. It seems I am a parasite living inside her,

The Bobsleigh Track

sucking all her blood. I also believe there's a fight between good and evil.

She is taking the hit on her physical health and we wrestle at times as I think she should put me on the shelf. Yet we both know since this winter journey has begun; the more we stay bonded in these hard times. Then, perhaps the end will be better for us both, perhaps my adult body does not really like her life. It seems like torture now as we are entwined in this cocoon of change. Yet what if I burst through her skin when I am fully grown Little One, what if I fully take over her skin and force that tough glass to break? What if it is not a dream but in the plan? What if she won't care how painful it was at book's end … .? It is hard though in this just over halfway point, to stay strong, after all, I am fully aware that this book and pen are now her most costly of items in every way. It is not something I take for granted and it seems appropriate to say thanks for letting me grow up inside. Thank you for loving me through the pain. I hope one day it will be worth it all, I hope one day you will be so pleased to see the Little One I am destined to be. What if my adult self, Alma and Sofia will have plenty of room in my new heart? After all, this is why I write, to put this wrong to right.

I mean who knows how big the human heart can grow? How much can skin stretch when it's healed from pain? I wonder could it be as big as a football pitch, or maybe even bigger again? How will I know unless I put it to the test? After all, this is not just about me. What about so many little ones out there who long to be free? Perhaps they are not little like me, i.e. a child. I wonder if they have been made little through man's mind. The little one of disability, the victims of adultery and selfish desire. Those who were not as fortunate as me. To little ones who did not know there was a bobsleigh to be borrowed for their race. Those who have no one cheering them on to the finish line for you, for us, for them, let the bobsleigh descend.

I do not like this, but I am done with running away. I am old enough now to see you can't take short cuts through snow globe glass without injury to yourself and others, in fact running away from pain only multiplies it and sometimes to the next generation. I see people out shopping, or watching a movie, or sitting on the beach, they can be very dressed up; they can look like they have it all. Yet, if you look closely for long enough, you can see little shards of glass. No matter how they try to run away, take more holidays, or buy a bigger house, the glass sliver simply won't go away. The longer it stays stuck in their flesh, the deeper the roots of glass take shape, what could have been treated immediately now is a lifelong scar, all because we have been conditioned to think it is wrong to cry, or be weak. Isn't it sad that we disconnect with pain, but demand more pleasure, passions and pursuits? This is what is hurting society not our glass roots.

I am now descending, just God and I; the snow is falling; the turns are quick. It is making my body feel quite queasy. Memories are flooding in where once held suppressed, it is like opening a bottle of prosecco it takes a while. Once the cork is popped the juices flow, this is how it is for me you know. I have told you before, but I will say it again. I cannot write in rhyme, but I will do my best as the motion of this bobsleigh is so unsteady and fast that my mind is trying so hard to stay focused on my task.

There is such freedom in writing not sticking to any plan. I am just allowing my pen to move as fast as it can. Sometimes I get embarrassed as writing is not my thing, but I can't get distracted by writings out there that are fit for a king. One thing I know for sure that I share with the many skilled authors out there, and that is the narrative that most child-centred books take. Most have a mix of good and bad, a hero, a victim, or a baddy inside, like the Big Bad Wolf, or the Wicked Witch of the West. Yet people still read these books aloud. I wonder is it because we find comfort in their pain, after all, life is not always full of sun rays and rainbows every day. It can bring us to our knees come what may. Even my favourite Ugly Duckling was bullied and tried, and some of the Bible stories Nana read to me have flashes of selfishness, greed and pride.

My bobsleigh is now making lots of twists and turns. It is like my life: it is how I learnt. You see, it is not just Hands that hurt my skin. I feel she has a team on her side. They don't use hands but that does not mean it does not leave scars. There are moments of unwelcoming glares from Hands' extended family who know I am not blood; I sometimes want to say: it is not my fault I'm here … you didn't see my dad came as a three. Him, my sister and little old me. I feel Hands has turned the tables of the care I once had on birth Mummy's side, or in dad's family's arms. She seems to write to tell them how I am, acting the caring parent. I can understand they don't come knocking at the door … after all, who would suspect she was not great to me? Her mood is so changeable, it is like an act and sadly they fall for her charm; if only they did not live so far away, I would run away I really would. I have tried to run away once before. I even threatened to jump off a bridge, but when Hands said go ahead, I do not care, I figured no one else would want me out there.

I even think my own dad sides with Hands in a way, although she never hurts me in front of him. He must know it is not good to go out all the time. He seems to go out every night, he doesn't stay home to care and be there. That's a woman's job in his eyes I guess … or maybe to stay and sense things were not right would cause an inconvenience to his plans, so he hands me over to the care of Hands. I am not meaning this to sound so rude, but really, she is a stranger in my home, forced on me and not my own. I long for my dad to take some time, so I practice my football every day. Hoping to have better skills, I would entice him to stay. He has some moments with me when he can be real, yet I find I help him back on track. I listen to his problems with Hands and pat him on the back. I know that my dad can't cope without my mum. So, I lower my voice about my own pain. If I have to get hurt so he has Hands, then

The Bobsleigh Track

I decide to hide my scars and my wounds. After all, he's my dad and I don't want to see him sad. The bobsleigh turns this time on a 90-degree edge. I nearly fall out, but that's what my life is all about.

Confusion, confusion and confusion once more. Am I loved? Do they care? What's the score? My body bolts upright in shock, my life seems it is just a bowl of pot luck. My memory is now recalling moments of family fun. My dad could be the funniest man. He loved to take us out for treats and meals. Hands seemed happy too, to have his time and these nights were fun. My dad would be the same when we went away, but I cannot stay on holiday every day, also I could not ever fully relax as Hands could get jealous, angry or mad at the slightest thing along the way. Yet, other times she could be relaxed and she encouraged me to have hobbies, she even gave her time. She would invite my friends over and make my life shine. It wasn't long before her hands and tongue erased the fun.

I cling onto God as my track spins out of control. I hear him whisper: it's OK Little One, I have got you; I won't let go. I open my eyes, I see God's back, he is looking and steering the bobsleigh down the track. I wish we weren't going so fast; I would like to just spend time on the side, but God is dealing with me so he can move inside. I would really like to see into God's eyes, but man has never seen God and stayed alive. He is too holy, too powerful, too mighty and pure, yet people paint God as distant and mean – when he is in fact the kindest man. Yet they blame all their suffering on God

Little One's Whisper

and his son, forgetting Jesus sweat drops of blood... his body broken and bruised for us. This negative view of God stops man seeing his love, don't you think God cries too? I do, he cries for moments alone with you.

Easter eggs have taken the word Easter off the box; man wants the chocolate without the pain. Oh, I am not saying abuse is ever right, but what about blaming Satan and the evil in man? There can't be sorrow without joy and heaven is a place where I long to be, after all, it says in heaven little ones will be free. The laughter, the sweetness of that day when heaven is their home, where no monsters stay.

As my bobsleigh takes another sharp turn, the runners are really starting to burn, the noise is loud, the pressure mounts. I move around from side to side – it is like I'm unlocking the pain deep inside. Hands and my dada married so fast. My dada didn't spend time with her family for long. Yet I've already figured it out. Hands' mum is exactly the same. I think this is how Hands got her name. She too, I believe, suffered the things that she does to me, which were sadly learnt on her own mother's knee. They both carry a controlling gene.

Hands' senior is a very good baker, she does it for church: Pavlovas, apple pies, to name a few. People line-up for her goods as she enters the pew. I have had many a taste of the skills of her hands. She is generous and goes overseas often to come home with lots of things for me. Yet when she minds me overnight on part of the holidays, I see there is more to this woman

The Bobsleigh Track

than she puts in her desserts. She can't relax she always wants to clean; I feel dirty when I come in from play. She will never shout, but I hear her complaining to Hands. I don't think unblood grandchildren were in her plan. Sometimes I sleep there when Hands and my dad fight. She just takes Hands' side and does not sit down to ask why. I guess if I raise a concern with my dad as I often do, she thinks I am being rude. I lie awake one long summer's night, anxiously waiting to be grown-up, when people like Hands' mum cannot come into my room and say: this is all your fault, look what you have done today.

My bobsleigh turns another turn, I can see the path is nearing an end. My shoulders begin to relax; I remember all the neighbours who were so kind to me when Hands was working part time. I used to get out as I couldn't stay when Hands senior was polishing the banister for the third time that day. I remember sitting alone, very early on a summer's day ... I felt like an orphan. I felt I didn't belong, sometimes I longed for summer to be gone. I think that is why I am never now bored as I made fun out of nothing ... I'd build dens with my bare hands, I even prepared funerals for dead birds in the fields, I laid them to rest with daisies and buttercups. I cleaned them up there as they were covered in mud. Then I took rides on milk floats, I bought mix-ups at the corner shop. Sometimes no one even knew if I got restless and needed somewhere new, so I would ride my bike to a very big park. No one would notice that I was gone and I took my sister often despite her protests. She rode her bike behind me, she did not want to come. Yet when we arrived, she would laugh and say ... "You were so brave to get us away."

*

When I go to bed sometimes, I feel I have done a day's work. I see the hurt, big ones carry in their heart and I try to nurse it. I try to fill their voids in my own wee ways while all the time hoping they say: it is OK we are better now. Yet what is even more shocking to confess is they would deny these wounds even as they undress. That's one of the reasons why I write; I don't want to minimise my pain and never repeat what happened to me, as most often this happens on a subconscious level in the mind. So, I am ripping out that broken film roll ... I will pull it out until there is nothing left until I am stripped bare, but please let me keep my thermal vest. I crawl towards forgiveness. I hope to forgive them all for stealing my worth, for making me feel I was not their own, or pushing me away when I was alone. This leads me to doubt my worth. I took this trauma and made it mine. I falsely believed the lies.

I can't say the Lord's Prayer today, there is more to my story, more hurts inside and I won't use religion to cover my pride, besides, I think God is tired of hearing prayers across the world echoing through glass. I think he would rather hear prayers one line at a time, whispered in his ear spoken in broken syllables through tears. Before I press on in my quest. I am aware

The Bobsleigh Track

of more pain I must address. These scars could later take over my life. Left untreated I then use them as excuses to retaliate with strife. What is really sad, is that deep down I still care for these people in a little way even though I never see them. I sometimes stop to hope they are OK; I have given up in the hope of an apology that's mine and yet. I want to say this to them, so I will write it down here. Maybe God will let it travel across the Irish Sea as they live too far to be seeing me.

I am sorry that life hurt you, I am sorry you have no one to tell, I don't want to punish you, yet I can't make you well. I hope if you ever read this, you will see this isn't about hurting you, or getting back at you. It is about freeing myself and loving myself as God's child, that's fact. You all are God's children as well, and I hope one day you surrender your scars to him and drink from his well. The unique monsters in your own unread stories are real and they won't disappear without looking them in the eye. God can help you with your own story if you let him. I hope you read it, I really hope you do, not just for me, not for my tears, but for your freedom and your deep fears.

The bobsleigh shudders to a squeaky stop, enough for now, enough, enough!

CHAPTER 13

Growing Pains

Then one day, will my very own heartbeat sound akin to a pure, unbroken masterpiece of Spanish a cappella?

Snow, snow, snow. Shake, shake, shake. The snow globe shudders. It's ferocious. I cling on, I slip, I fall. I get up. The pattern repeats. I have mastered all kinds of standing skills. I can even do it on one leg, yet when my snow globe is lifted by some hand, the shaking slips me to terror. I am like a spider trying to get out of a ceramic bath. I hear people saying hurry up, come on, albeit in my mind. Yet no one understands I can barely stand, let alone write, all my attempts are often futile. It has snowed every day for three months; it is the worst blizzard yet. I would scream if I thought it would help.

Alone ... I feel alone and lack energy to even build a snowman or ice skate. I am weak, maybe the weakest yet. I ache. Alone I stand. I fall. I shift the shadows. I raise my head. I see further, I see pain, not just my pain but pain. I am able to read pain like people play the piano without music. It is natural to me, but it hurts. It is not something I can talk to my friends about. Thankfully I love mischief and humour. We get busy. The night falls. The curtains are drawn and the lights go out. The snow is still falling, I do not understand why it won't stop. I want out of here.

My heart thumps. My fingers turn white and I

distract myself watching winter sports on TV. The bobsleigh is still there, Alma, Sofia, are you there? Are you still inside me for the ride? I am not used to using both hands to cling onto God. I know Sofia has climbed inside. I hear her arranging memory files in my mind and rewiring my trauma hardware storage. Setting my tear ducts on defrost setting. Alma, oh, I feel Alma. It is like my skin is receiving a back to front massage, she holds my strained muscles, she soothes the spasms and tends to my wounds. Alma is working on my body, my mind and my emotions. I imagine her sprinting around my body, she is always singing or humming, today she is chanting like she is an up-and-coming New York City rapper: Snow, snow, snow. Shake, shake, shake. Don't give up till this glass dome can break.

She is looking for the words to release me, I wonder does she weave them together? Does she collect them from places within that I don't even know hurt? She knows the full story after all and is qualified to piece it together. My Alma is so in tune with my unique way to release my pain, I believe everyone has their own Alma. Their own Alma is waiting to tour around their body. To pull back the trauma and perhaps reveal, that through art or display, the exhibits of heartache in an encased cabinet in life's museum. Or perhaps your Alma is awaiting the right moment that your skin is ripe for peeling. Alma waits to undress your battle armour of skin. She wants to see the raw internal state of your being. The parts you hide, the parts that bleed.

Alma, I appreciate your encouraging cheers, but

please can you stop rapping now, please. Alma finishes her last line, as if to complete the chorus is igniting more power than stopping halfway. That is what she constantly reminds me to do with my writing. She pushes me to completion. It is quiet but I hear a distant creak, a clink, a pause. Alma has lifted the needle of the vinyl record player within. We all have our own life's music collection stored inside, each song links to a season, an occasion, a year, a longing, a loss or a moment of delight. Each song that makes it to the filing shelf is of meaning and purpose. Alma has selected one of my nana's tunes, a song that my nana played and prayed over me. I cannot recognise any song from its introduction of melody alone, yet with the first chord I freeze. I am frozen in time. An ice sculpture entranced in nothing but this moment. The song was written for a dying child in 1862, yet today it is bringing the dead things to life: *Jesus Loves Me*.

As the music continues to wash over me, I release tears, they naturally defrosted so quickly. They are flooding my body and bathing my heart in healing. I bow my head and repeat the only part of the Lord's Prayer I can say with truth, "Our Father, who art in heaven, hallowed be thy name; thy kingdom come; thy will be done on earth as it is in heaven."

Heaven? How can God's will be done on earth as it is in heaven? I wonder, am I being too adventurous, daring and idealistic. I then pause and think on heaven. Everyone wants to go there. Even if they don't believe in it. They still collect feathers and anything that reminds them of an afterlife. They can't help themselves – we are born for heaven. I am not sure if heaven will be literal or non-literal. Perhaps I see ... heaven as a place of beauty, a beauty that will require all of eternity to be unravelled, as we would be too overwhelmed if it emerged all at once. I see stunning aesthetic beauty: waterfalls and meadows, beaches and rainforests. The seasons as we know them destroyed, there will be no need for winter, autumn or spring. A constant summer. Blazing love, dining with loved ones, complete in peace as our pain on this earth will melt away as we look into the very eyes of our God. If Christ lives in us, we too have heaven within. Isn't that the part of us that the Holy Spirit fans into flame? Isn't it the part of us that longs for social justice, purity and unity?

I wonder how many people know the Lord's Prayer, yet have never dined on heaven on earth, in their home or relationships? For me, Little One, God's will being done for me, is to release me from bondage. I know that. I know that I am being led to face my pain, heal, then share my healing.

I see people walking around the bobsleigh tracks. Good people, but people jumped out of the bobsleigh when life's hurt became too much. They still love God; they just didn't await their day of deliverance. I know God travels in thousands of millions of bobsleighs, saying it is never too late to travel intimately with me, and give me your addiction, grief or pain. I suspect I too will need to catch the bobsleigh again in time. Perhaps at times throughout the remainder of my life.

Growing Pains

Double. Double sounds fun: double choc-chip cookies, double pillows, double-decker buses, double ice-cream cones. Yet for me double is not nice. I have a double fight on my hands for my voice to be heard. My double fight: part one, I live in a snow globe; part two, my snow globe is stored in an ever-weakening adult body. I can only write when my snow globe is not being shaken and when my adult body can be still. Sometimes I wake my adult body at 6am to write, sometimes I keep her awake at night, simply to comfort me. I am trying to rebirth myself through Little One. My adult body nurses me, hears me and believes in me, she has consciously carried me for two years. Like most pregnant mothers she is tired. The intensity is building. I am in big school now, my body is growing, accept my feet as they are still tiny. My voice is growing stronger. I am taking up much more room within. I had never expected it to be so painful for us both. At times I ache, she aches, it aches. No baby showers are organised, very few know she is carrying. In fact, even we do not know aside from our faith, if this birthing will ever reach the time of delivery. It is a place of suspended hope. A place of waiting, of hurting, healing, breaking and strengthening.

My adult body is human. She reaches breaking points. I hear her saying I want to give up. Give up on me? I do not want that. How could she? She shouts. I hide, she seeks, I wait, she comes. We share tender moments once again. We connect. She whispers I am sorry, I love you. I whisper it is OK, I love you too.

Little One's Whisper

There is an intimate knowing. We need each other – I the growing, learning child, her the imperfect, broken human, yet our greatest need is to be carried in the arms of God. With pregnancy the mother and baby have separate blood supplies, so with this our blood supply is one. One day if I grow up, all that will be left of my adult body is a deflated pile of skin. That skin will become my scarf, I will wear this scarf to remind myself of the sacrifice; my full growth would require her consumption. I thought my healing would be found in having my adult body acting as a substitute for my own mother. But in fact, my healing will remove her and leave me, Little One, standing in wholeness and strength alone.

My development is dependent not on her, but on her willingness to allow me to outgrow her. As with natural pregnancy, an inward tug of war exists over nutrients and blood flow. The same is true for us. Although in our uniqueness we are the same, the same blood, the same heart, the same body. I need her in time to let me go fully and allow me to be the living, viable, strong healthy adult. Then one day, will my very own heartbeat sound akin to pure, unbroken masterpiece of Spanish a cappella resounding across the Mediterranean Ocean with boldness and without apology. Oh, I am only a child and on this I do wonder?

Isn't it ironic my healing will be the very origins of my original and ever-threading pain of losing my own birth mother; double-loss, double-healing. In the here and now, I grieve the loss of the adult body that carries

Growing Pains

me. She is dying as I've overcome her. Her body has been broken since I lifted my pen. Her body is breaking. I hear her cry in pain, I hide my pen. I feel guilt when she travels to the hospital. I was sad when she was put to sleep for surgery. I was scared when she lost all her wisdom teeth one by one. I have almost wanted to emigrate when she has suffered friends not understanding her social decline, her reduced finances for one reason or another. I hid inside her, when her car exploded and when she crawled on the bathroom floor with another infection, after another; these moments are simple snapshots of this painful transition. Only God knows the true extent.

Even doctors are limited in their healing power, after all, I don't show up on X-rays. There are helpers sent along, but sometimes those who she thought would help are the ones she feels judged by. Often the biggest help comes from unrecognised faces and acts of humanity are extended from passers-by who know little. To those people I thank you. It is painful but we are called to die to self, according to John 3:30, "He must become greater, I must become less."

I, Little One, am a vessel for his increase. Human comfort has been removed in many ways, after all, this bobsleigh journey is ours alone and when my mind struggles to comprehend it all, Sofia arises. Proverbs 3:5–6, "Trust in God with all your heart, lean not on your own understanding; in all your ways acknowledge him and he will make clear your path."

The bobsleigh shudders to begin the second journey.

The destination here is Painsville. A letter awaits in an envelope, it reads ... My growing pains.

*

I walk into the room. I don't feel safe. There is a monster in here. In fact, sometimes there are many monsters. Only I know they are monsters as they wear pretty masks, so no one else knows. I see through masks. They are not six-foot black monsters. They are not the type of villains depicted in fairy tales, but they are monsters. They don't stomp around the hallways wrecking the house with every step. They do not shout 'Fee-fi-fo-fum!', or wait until the lights go out to appear. They are normal. They drink tea and bake cakes and laugh. They work. They shop. They even go to church and are pleasant to their neighbours.

The room in Hands senior's house scares me in a different way. There is no shouting. But I am not blood – of their blood. I sense I do not belong. The truth is I don't and that I was never asked did I want to belong to their blood. It takes time to grow, trust, even with safe grown-ups. But my history and present have been re-written – no one mentions my roots, there's no talk of Nana or Annie love. My dad, too, is a fully fledged member of this new club. I am slightly older and I feel that I have been kidnapped into a world that scares me. I suspect my dad, too, feels scared walking into this beautifully presented room, full of fine furniture and ornaments. I suspect he too would prefer the open fire

Growing Pains

with simple furniture and sentimental keepsakes. Yet he allows this room to swallow him, in allowing that, I am left from the mouth of a monster.

Monsters sounds extreme. Yet how would you describe people who subtly push you out? Blame you for Hands and Dad's domestic violence when alone with them. How would you describe people who try to talk about your shortcoming in code; don't they see, I know the code? I learnt it years ago. My interpretation of that coded language is this is broken love. Perhaps it is all they know, but it hurts. It leaves a void, sometimes I don't even want sweets or cakes there. Sometimes I am crying inside. I get bought gifts. I am dressed in clothes like a toy. I am a toy to them. A toy they tire of.

My dad's family live far away beside Aunt Annie, we still go but it is becoming less. My grandad is now in a home with dementia. Yet he never forgets to give me a five-pound note when I visit. I know most children would dream about what they would buy with this money, yet all I want to buy him are his newspapers and some eggs so he can pretend he is on the chicken run. I stare out the window, I know I am different, very different. I have a lump in my throat. I am a child and I do not understand why old people are left in care homes. All I know is he has nothing tonight aside from his Bible and he always likes being alone with this book. It's ironic though as the Bible clearly states we should honour those who are weak. Grandad is now forced into his own snow globe, no wife, no daughter and now only rare visits from my sister and Little One.

My Birth Mummy had no brothers or sisters to help Grandad. I know people say he is well looked after as he cannot remember now and needs nurses. He remembers me, I see it in his eyes. Who gives a stranger a five-pound note and reaches out for their hand? I think he wanted me – to go with me to check on the chickens. He wants to feel love and smell familiarity. I wonder does Grandad choose to forget things at times. To block the pain of losing his only daughter and wife within six years. It is a sad day when a man goes out of this world in time, clutching a book that teaches a better way. I wish he just had one chicken to tuck in tonight.

His funeral comes and goes in a flash. After the funeral Annie said to me in her famous kitchen; "look at your lovely clothes. I could never provide this for you." In reality I think she was saying; "I am handing you over fully into the care of Hands and Daddy now." On this car ride home, the lump in my throat was so painful. I forced it to the back of my throat with the force of a strong volley. In time the lump ruptured into tears as we crossed the bridge. I wept. Aunt Annie had not died, our bond hadn't died in part. The car kept moving, no one addressed my pain. Perhaps in doing so they would be forced to admit that a child grieves. I got passed some sweets and offered a colouring book. Yet I was nil by mouth and only interested in the black crayon. This night changed my heart shape. I think to grieve what is still alive is harder than to grieve what is gone.

Growing Pains

So, I fight alone in this room. Sometimes I try too much and aim to win their affections especially with Hands' brother and his wife who barely say hello. Interestingly, even though, I am not fully welcome here, I can sleep upstairs when babysitting is needed. I am grateful that the cooking is good, although no photo of me hangs, unlike at Annie's where an animal pom-pom I made resides on her dressing table in a zip and seal bag of honour. I guess I am simply glad that here my skin is not bruised. I have had so many lovely moments too, when this wasn't the case. Especially when Hands' father smiled gently, he is a nice enough man. Yet a man is not a man who is under the control of a woman. My dad can be selfish with his time and love is not selfish. That too makes him a monster sometimes in my eyes, as he is not checking over the castle where his princess lives. He is absent a lot of the time. When he is here, this is not really love. He knows. He silences the knowing as it is done behind his back. But I suspect he knows. He is just not strong enough to devour his own grief monster and rebuild a life that is better suited for his little one.

Guilt and shame rise, should I silence these thoughts and simply focus on the peaceful seasons? The friends who come to play and sleep over in those times, the meals out, the holidays, playtime. I have it good a lot too. Yet I do not think it's right to have monster moments at all. I should feel safe all the time and be able to tell of the monster teacher at school who repeats often to me: "You are a lame brain, mutton ejit, black and almond, pink spotted, salt and vinegar flavoured nerd." Surely my home, this room, should be a sanctuary from a child's cruel exposure to the sinful world. Again, I fight this alone. I become bad to keep grown-ups scared of coming too close to me.

Hands is becoming more subtle, more skilled at minimising and denying me full ownership of my house. Oh my house! My dad and my worth. When I watch TV downstairs, she thinks nothing of turning it over to *Countdown*, after all, she tells me is that I don't pay the TV Licence. I go to my room; I have a TV in there. In ways my own room is my home. That does not stop her bursting in uninvited and verbally or physically attacking me. But it reduces it. Then I am safe outside, at my friends' houses, in the cul-de-sac and in their gardens. I am extending my den. I need more space and Hands doesn't know where my den is. She doesn't play, my dad doesn't either, it is all mine.

Hands gets jealous when I go to my old babysitter's house now. Or maybe she is scared, either way I am told to make excuses to come home. They can't understand why I would leave halfway through a World Cup match. I make excuses. My life is excuse after excuse. Subtle hurts no one notices. But I do. My birthday card only gets to stay up for one day to make room for Christmas cards, really it says attention back on the queen.

Hands has new toys now, two nieces. They are at my house most days. She prefers her upgraded toys. They have their own yogurt shelf in the fridge. Violent outbursts are spared, yet I watch how she needs them to need her. Her dirty looks say so much to me, her harsh

Growing Pains

eyes. Her controlling spirit, her OCD cleaning and lack of laughter. She is skilled at slapping and kissing me at the same time and this confuses my thoughts and guilts me into acceptance. My thoughts reassess. Hands kicked my sister up the hall today. She was shouting at her about her messy room and accusing her of lying and being silent. My assessment outcome – injustice. I grab her by her arm and pull her off with all my might. In a flash she forgets her grievance with Dolly. My sister from here on is named Dolly. She looks like a doll.

Dolly doesn't fight back. I stand up for us both. I don't want to hurt her. I never attack first. But I do all I can to police the situation. It's survival. It's perhaps wrong. I feel bad afterwards but what else can I do? She kicks, slaps, pulls me by the hair to chairs and bangs my head off the walls. I can't change the behaviour, no one can. I try to love her in between. I feel sorry for her wounded hands. Yet when I am in attack mode I simply try to live and ease my sister's skin. Painsville – destination complete for now. I bow my head and weep.

*

Like any child my attention is diverted to an 80's Double Dip sherbet packet. One candy stick attached to cherry and separate orange sherbet sachet. I have plenty of sweets, collecting them for midnight feasts is my favourite hobby.

Alma and Sofia arise and guide my hand, they point to God's weeping over me. This was never his fault. I accept that they teach me how to make double fun. They show me to continually dip into my favourite orange side. The cherry side they say is better not to be detached from the packet. You should never detach from pain. The cherry sherbet section represents all your painful experiences; you need to learn to befriend it as part of your story. However, you need to choose not to allow it to tempt you to dip in repeatedly to its life-stealing flavour. You need to own the pain. Rather that you befriend it, but chose not to allow it to tempt you into its life-stealing flavour thereby owning it.

The orange side has life-giving power it soothes you and reminds you that you are loved not forgotten and an adopted child of God. Thy will is being done on earth as it is in heaven – no story spoken or unspoken is too great for heaven to burst into and cover in sherbet. I suspect I will be eating sherbet for some time. Dipping into wounds, dipping out with healing. It is the double dip. I dip in and out of the sherbet, as I post the letter of this part of my life back to sender. This sherbet is still sold today. It can't be substituted. Its name is Jesus. If he can heal me, he can heal all little ones, I think upon the *Jesus Loves Me* song. This song is not just for me, I believe Jesus loves you, just as you are. Jesús te ama tal como eres.

CHAPTER 14

Robin Bird

God speaks through his extraordinary act of creation into every paper cut etched upon our hearts.

Alive but broken, suspended between the noise of other's joy, their tangible delight that they display without apology or perhaps even awareness. They walk through the hallways of my mind spraying their perfume of life's delights into my dark chamber. Their tales of travels, their new chapters of promises fulfilled. The bigger home. The release of period pain, exchanged by a new zest for life. That life I know is not built on the foundation of God's love, that life, the chasing ... the longing will all come to an abrupt end when, without warning, death knocks on the door and it ceases in seconds.

God, I am left exposed to the harsh realities of winter and struggling to create with the only fruits on my table, red berries. I can't even eat them, but simply slice them in politeness for the robins and lay them down on the bird table each night. Wolves ... Arctic wolves surround me in my fight to pursue God's destiny for my life. My cuts seem to act as a magnet for their insatiable appetite to devour my soul and rob me of all I own ... my simple faith in Christ. The gnashing of their teeth, the drool of their mouths suspends me in fear. A paralysis unseen by the human eye. A deep grief. A longing. I simply want to know will winter ever end for me? Will I once again dance on the dance floor of life? Or will my faith in God forever keep me locked away from joy? Oh, I know the Bible reassures me repeatedly about God's faithfulness. Yet in the waiting, in the unknown, in the void. Can you, my God, heal my pain? Can you be my everything?

Perhaps I will not even desire the world's pleasures when I have experienced and hugged summer. As painful as the winter season is, it is revealing two truths to me: firstly nothing can ever separate you, or me from God's love, and secondly only in him can you and I be whole. Wolves continue to encircle me, ripping at my flesh. What hurts me the most is not that the wolves are evil – I am in knowledge of that, yet the stabbing pains in my stomach come as a result of not receiving an instant release. God, why do you allow this wait? Perhaps you are using this time to lift my eyes off my idols. After all, anything I place before you is an idol. The waiting humbles me, it exposes my impatience, my need to be in control. I do not believe God sends the wolves, but I do believe at times he permits them, yes. On nights like tonight, I really wish the wolf of death did not capture my mum. I was only ten months old. Yet I acknowledge God is the author of my story, he sees a greater narrative. I bow my head to the sovereignty of God. Job 1:21 "Naked I came from my mother's womb, and naked I will depart. The Lord gave and the Lord has taken away, may the name of the Lord be praised."

I look up from my gaze out of the snow globe window of despair. Robins … look at these robins. How do they endure winter, singing their dawn chorus and humming their goodnight lullabies? I am dazzled by their red breasts, entranced by their delicate ethereal beauty. My Alma is soothed by the strength of their chorus, their blissfully happy countenance, despite it being winter. Maybe robins know more than us humans about how to live. I wonder do they stand on the morning shores, or enjoy sunset tweeting?

As I continue to try and continue with the Lord's Prayer the next line reads, "Give us this day our daily bread," I suspect this is their line of preference. After all, they can't order food online, or do the weekly shop. They can't even visit a food bank in difficult times. No, they are totally dependent upon God to stir the mealworms, to ripen the berries and ignite passion in the hearts of gardeners to lay banquets on the bird tables nationwide. They know more than many humans the need for total reliance upon God. On an emotional level they fly rigorous journeys, until their eyes weep of wind burn, to simply connect to loved birds further afield. They don't simply tweet on social media forgetting the profound healing and connection that can only be sourced beak to beak. They bridge the gender gap with both male and female sporting the infamous red breast.

Oh, robin bird, I wish I was you. I wish I could fly away without thought or care. You captivate me little Petirrojo (Spanish for robin). I think I love you robin bird. In fact, I do. Can you stay with me for a while? My heart is heavy and Alma, Sofia and God seem silent. I wonder why in my moment of need I find solace in a bird? No offence little robin, but you are not human or divine. Yet I sense in moments of deep trauma and grief does not creation gently whisper God's vision of Sofia, to carefully echo love into Alma through the senses? I know deep connection is found in prayer in the word of God and through worship. Yet I feel sometimes the heart is too broken to speak and therefore God speaks through his extraordinary act of creation into every paper cut etched upon our hearts. The comfort blanket of the ocean lapping at the shore, the warm hug of the sun, the bird's song, the butterfly kisses, the smell of fresh flowers and the taste of sweet grapes. Doesn't creation demonstratively say: my child, I love you. Your father, God. Oh, and the seasons. The seasons punctuate our circumstances, transient and fleeting unlike our God who changes not.

Oh robin, do you see my paper cuts? They ache. I do not have a home. I feel guilty to mention this as I get spoilt with clothes, holidays and ice-cream sundaes. I know other little ones don't. Yet I can't ignore the subtle displacement from my nest. The jealousy of Hands that pushes me to a corner, that somehow creates room for her chicks of choice. Her nieces, her nephews and her friends, all of whom don't witness her rage. Her uncontrolled bursts of anger, shouting and put downs. My dad, he is often absent from my nest either in body, or in mind. So, robin, I fledged my nest mentally, far too young. Oh, I sleep here, but accept every offer of a sleepover anywhere with anyone. I started working in a coffee shop last week aged 13. I stand independent. I am alone somehow, don't be deceived by other nest displays, trimmed in Laura Ashley twigs and laced in fancy bed linen. Many clean, sparkling nests are not fit for purpose, they house, but do not home.

Oh, robins they are such good parents. They tirelessly build nests and look after their offspring until they are fully ready to flee the nest. Even then, they search for food for them, until they are fully able to navigate the world alone. The male robins doing the feeding, the female robin preparing a fresh nest for her next brood. Don't you see grown-ups, if tiny robins make new nests, why do you think it is OK to force non-blood family together without proper support? I'm not broken – my nest is, my dad blinded. His blindness causes pain. Firstly, in his lack of emotional presence, secondly in his blind-eyed approach to my systemic terrorised exposure to an authority figure I call mum. A mum is more than a word. I've tried to bond; part of me loves Hands. But I hate her actual hands; they inflict hurt. It's living in a war of attrition. It is like a constant game of charades, a game I am too young to fully understand.

A game, a dangerous game of adults parenting in and through their own emotional bondage. Oh, I do have compassion for them, but it does not make it OK. If robins can display such selfless parenting skills, then shouldn't grown-ups? Shouldn't they open their eyes to the reality of broken homes on innocent children's lives. For you, for us, for them, I raise my little voice. It's not good enough. It's just not. So little robin, can you sit with me a while longer, can you lick my wounds, can you be my friend? Oh, and robin bird I love your red breast. I wonder how you got it. I've heard a legend that you picked a thorn from Jesus' crown as he hung on the cross on Good Friday. I've heard that as the blood poured it stained your breast. I wonder robin bird, is there any truth in this tale. Could your species of bird be marked for all eternity with one encounter with Jesus? It may be a tale, but I see truth in it.

We, his children, have red breasts of hearts that can only be whole, healed and redeemed with Christ's sacrifice of blood for us. Jesus' passion, his sacrifice his unbearable suffering. This atonement from God to allow us to be free to fly from the bondage of sin and oppression. This spilling of blood creates the perfect nest, as it adopts us into God's family. It is our home here at the foot of the cross. Robin where are you going? Please stay. I can't Little One, my job is done.

As the little robin departs its evening chorus of singing is loud enough to be heard over mountains and seas. As I wave goodbye to my robin bird. I ask God to give me this day my daily bread.

CHAPTER 15

Raw War

Hurt has a root. It is a poisonous weed in our society. It can be choked to death by the outpouring of unconditional love.

War spelt backwards is raw.

I would like to argue when we feel raw, we are dealing with an aspect of war conditions.

It is raw to face loss.

It is raw to be injured.

It is raw to be subjected to ill health, to lose a limb, an organ, or the hope of healing of emotions.

This is my theory, anything raw is war, war is raw.

You may not agree with my equation. That is OK. This is not a fact; it is just my theory. War is brutal, relentless and bloody. I do not think any war from the beginning of time has not been fought under snow globe conditions. Then that snow globe is placed on the mantelpiece, glorified, idolised, and even worshiped. Oh, I too have respect for the fallen soldiers of the First and Second World Wars, and I too remember them. But honestly, I am more concerned with the trauma still being felt because of these wars. The wounded soldiers, the broken homes, the mental-health crisis. The simple cost that did not end on the beaches of Dunkirk, rather it has set a raw, ticking clock that would tick through the second, third and fourth generations. The Second World War never truly ended, its consequences remain.

Little One's Whisper

Make-do and mend was the attitude of home making, but I wonder was it too the attitudes we still feel today? The lessons passed through the years that whisper make-do with pain, try and mend the cracks. Come on, stiffen your upper lip and "keep calm and carry on."

This next generation has been labelled the snowflake generation, seen as less resilient. Yet I would like to commend the Millennials for being naked with their pain. For allowing thick skin to be thawed. To be exposed in this uncertain world where words like Trump, global warming and Brexit hit them before their morning coffee. They know what mental health means, good isn't it? But uncomfortable for us, so we start a name-calling war to silence them into the history of being seen and not heard. More comfortable, isn't it?

War started and finished in a snow globe. Liberation and winning is only an illusion. Hate has an insatiable appetite. Do you really believe that hate can be fed and satisfied by one war? There are no winners from war. Even if a country wins, wounded soldiers' lives are forever frozen in time by the magnitude of the trauma. So, more walls are built to protect their pain as they hope their snow globe country is the most dominant, the biggest, and the most influential. Yet all snow globes are fragile, and I question national pride when God holds the country's snow globe in his hand. Like a toy in the hand of its creator. No country is bigger than God. We are just so proud; pride is the war within hearts that needs blowing up.

Raw War

*

What about my raw war? It is not fought in trenches or televised, no, some raw wars are simply fought in homes, in hearts and minds. Behind walls of brick, decorated in twinkly lights. I never wanted to be conscripted into war. I am now conscription age but I still feel too young, so alone, I take my position on the front line of battle. War? What war I hear you mutter, you have God, Alma and Sofia by your side, that will secure your sweet victory. I do not feel like I have connections to these sources in this war. I have turned my back on God. Do not misunderstand me, I am not an atheist; I cannot deny God's presence, I sense Alma and Sofia close by too. But I silence them like I have been silenced. I lock them inside and bind them in barbed wire. It is my war and win it I will, and alone.

As I raise my fist, I pause, I wonder is there a better way? A better way to deal with the injustice of Hands and the subtle way dad ignores my emotional needs. I feel prompted to expose the domestic wrongdoing, their sporadic violence against one another. Hands' outbursts overpower dad's strength, I wonder if he is actually more colluded to Hands than I see. It is not clear. He says he loves me; he gives me lifts for socials but a greater distance has emerged. I wonder if it is because I am now 17 and he is done fighting with Hands for my rights. Maybe it is him who has conscripted me into this war. He now a veteran. I wish I could seek help for all concerned, but who would help me seriously? Would a man of the cloth help me when it is not a Sunday? Would a policeman help me when there are paramilitaries running the streets of Northern Ireland? So, I conclude swiftly that adults in society are inept at dealing with domestic wars. They are too bloody messy!

I get busy, I make a war plan. First I am going to start with negotiation and peace talks. I prepare my concerns into mental files and walk towards the dining table. Have you noticed that all 'talks' take place round the table, it seems to provide an instant wooden wall of defence. Hardly conducive to open conversation. I freeze, I have not sat at the dining table in least a year; I have only been eating sporadically at home and tend to use the kitchen table. It has become evident that the welcome is not overly forthcoming for anything else. Dolly often joins me. It is like we are not worthy to dine on the Sunday dinner table. A subtle but powerful rejection.

So, avoiding mealtime, I enter the living room that seems unfamiliar to my domestic territory. I sit on the brown leather chair that faces a glass window. The patio flowers falsely pristine behind the glass. Dad and Hands take position on the three-seater sofa against the wall. The walls drip of terracotta paint and nothing is out of place as the cushions act as mere display items rather than enhancing comfort. Their sofa has three spaces, but Hands sits on the arm of the sofa. It non-verbally shouts: it's two against one. I feel as cold as ice. The TV is still blurring and it's *Countdown*. I watch the vowels and consonants being pulled out and

Raw War

I wish I could invent a word that captures the intensity of my inner raw emotional state. Unable, I simply say this is not working. Can we fix this? I offer some examples of why I believe we are in a war zone surrounded by toy soldiers. This is met with hostility, denial and attack. Hands storms off in her car, Dad follows in his. I sit alone, my head in my hands. Peace talks closed, failed. Over!

So, I move on, like many countries I run away from the problems I face. I am spinning swirling and shaking inside my snow globe. My snow globe music is no longer playing my familiar melody of sound. Rather it is blasting music from my nightclub, boom, boom, boom, the intensity rises. The lights flash quicker, the ice melts and I am warm and free on the platform of my own life. I wait. I am not certain; I do not feel this is very safe. But I am lured into the lights, my clarity dazzled by the brightness and I am desperately attracted to a momentary change in my circumstances. Due to noise levels I can no longer converse with friends. My chest bounces inside its cavity, it resounds its vibrations throughout my body. I begin to lose myself in the strobe lighting, tranced by the fleeting change of colours. The smoke rises, it gives the impression of everyone else dancing in slow motion. I feel euphoric. I knock back drink after drink, shot after shot. The dance floor camouflages my need for sexualised contact with men, or maybe the drugs I have taken tell me that. I feel disgusting cheap and shameful, yet simultaneously I feel happy, free and exciting. I am not sure which feelings are correct, so I numb my thought process with more alcohol, more cigarettes and more drugs. My snow globe is frozen in this moment.

I feel God's voice urging me back into his protective arms once more. I refuse. I won't surrender. Not a bone of me. My soul Alma is crushed, curled in the corner of my snow globe, weakened from this toxic poison. Sofia's wisdom is there every time I order another drink. But I do not care. Do you hear me? I do not care. I just want liberation and I have found it on this dance floor. The music comes to an abrupt end. The dimmed lights turned onto full power. We are told to leave in that moment I sense this is not the lasting solution. I am searching for. But it will do. Make-do and mend is the war cry after all.

I do not want morning to arrive. I wake in a mascara-drenched pillow, complete with smudges of fake tan. My feet are red raw from my high heels. I am still party dressed. I shower away the smoky smell and my guilty memories and clothe myself in reality once more. I pull back my icy curtains, I still see snow. I know my choices are not healing this raw war, but they are numbing my pain.

Can I remind you I feel I had no real choices, I was conscripted into their war. I up my game, albeit subconsciously. I will engage in a protest of hunger striking. I don't avoid food because I think I am fat – because I'm very thin – I stop eating to harm myself rather than my perceived enemy. This raw war I now carry into my stomach. I'd simply rather fight it there than in my hands. I get thinner and thinner. I'm anorexic and fading away. My dear friend breaks through my mental block, she calls or visits every day. She partners in my pain. You see, I've retreated to bed. I have not risen in four months, except to shower or go out to a nightclub. I have dropped out of university and, even though I have had a part-time job since I was 13, I have made myself redundant. I am semi-dead.

I am drained of a love supply and exhausted by my lack of parental involvement. Except for my angelic friend, there are no truce offers drawn up. No knocks on my door. No acknowledgement of my suffering. But my angelic friend changes my war plan. Today she has arrived with food and ordered me to start healing, bite by bite, no matter how small. Thank you, dear Dorothy.

Slowly I beat my new enemy anorexia and I feel I've escaped potential death. Angel friend my love for you is eternal. Now I've flourished into a young woman I feel Hands subconsciously treats me as a sexual threat. It is as though my mother's scent chokes her and my mother's pale eyes reflect in mine and this blinds her reason. Maybe I try to stay so thin to shrink my breast, to delay my period arriving, it still is not here. I wonder if I try to remain childlike. I do not know how to fix your jealousy Hands. I am not a sexual threat especially with my own father. I am simply starving for fatherly love.

I have no weapons, only my hands. So, my hands now fight Hands directly. I never strike first, but when my head is smashed against bathroom tiles and my blood spills, I push through the door. I scream abuse and try to shake her into normality. I do not know if Hands is really stronger than me or not, but she always wins. I think she wins because really I am not engaging in war to harm her, rather I am simply acting in self-defence. These fights arise over trivia, yet the raw war feels deeply spiritual. It is like she is controlled by a force that is trying to choke me and everything I represent. To force me to be a refugee, no longer feeling confined to only my bedroom. No, she wants me homeless. She even invades my bedroom territory for attacks. My heritage is threatened, the legacy of my mother stolen and a right to my father's love is reduced to staged moments when often there is a thaw and flickers of surrender. But the war runs deep, it will again arise. I wish someone had told me before that we fight on a much deeper level than just below the skin's surface. Ephesians 6:12 "For our struggle is not against flesh and blood, but against the rulers, against the authorities, against the powers of this dark world and against the spiritual forces of evil in the heavenly realms."

Don't you see, in raw war any war is not human against human, country against country? It's evil against good. It's been the only war worthy of our attention. Sin needs to be defeated and broken souls mended. So, they do not need to rage war. Yet we glorify war, don't we? Many argue that the Second World War was just, but I wonder was a war that killed over 50 million people the only way to resolve this crisis? Oh, but what about saving the Jews, well that was not the UK or US's priority. Many Jewish refugees were left afloat on the seas, unwelcome in safer lands.

Europe dissolved into crisis after the Second World War with the erection of the Berlin Wall and Eastern European came under Soviet control, which welcomed the cold war and saw Europe divided by the Iron Curtain. The Wall eventually came down, but we built more walls. Brexit could build even more walls to keep nationality strong minus immigrant influence. It has divided British people into two camps: the 52 per-cent leavers and the 48 per-cent remainers. Yet our problem is bigger than Europe, it is a global problem of the shunning of God's standards and I see our problems fixed only by surrendering our pride to the war against sin. I am neither in the remain or leave camp, with Brexit it is a lonely stance, I just want peace. Do not be distracted by this generational issue. The solution to humanity's problems globally is much more complex than the European Union. Brexit is simply a micro-war within a massive war, when the only war worth fighting for is the establishment of tolerance and love dispelling racism and hate.

*

I lower my raw war pride and, once again, surrender my pain to Christ; Hands got her way, she asked me to move out and never return home. I walk down the street pulling along two suitcases. I asked my friend to take me in for a while. She arrived promptly. Hands came running up to us as we loaded my suitcases into the car. Hands said, "Little One is too much for her to manage." My friend replied, "What is too much for you to handle is the truth. Little One asked you to be kinder to Dolly. She called you out on your poor behaviour. You're hell-bent on not changing. Your war is not with Little One, your war is with yourself."

I am sorry God, Alma and Sofia. Please forgive me for my ignorance and failings. Please forgive our nation for glorifying war. For opposing immigrants when we are all immigrants. We have all migrated from our mother's womb to this world, before migrating again to heaven. Exhausted, I fall asleep. Please give me a dream God, show me your way to win the war. I do not dream vividly, or in colour, as I often do. Rather the words of a familiar song resound in my head: *To Dream the Impossible Dream.*

I have looked a soldier in the eye, down the barrel of a gun, crossing the Irish borders. I have had war forced into my bloodline; I tear down this war in my mind. I refuse to accept war is the only way. God, in my defeated state, rescue me. I hand this battle over to your care. I am not sure what the star represents in the above song, but I imagine it as the same star seen by the Wise Men. The star that leads and is still leading people to Christ. Once more I pray. I am sending out an SOS. Send out your army of angels, find me, please never stop marching for my cause.

For our cause, for their cause, fix the raw places in

me, fix the raw places in others, then the need for war will diminish. Begin at home, raw hurt has a root. I do not believe hurtful actions and behaviours can breed across cultures and continents of those who have had their hearts planted securely in love and belonging, do you? Hurt has a root, it is a poisonous weed in our society. It can be choked to death by the outpouring of unconditional love.

You may not have in your garden shed the means to cure this raw hurting world, but you have the resource within your shed to begin in the soil of your own heart, even if it is just a small patch begin there. Kill the weeds of rawness on your own land. Then, if you are brave enough, recruit yourself into the army of healing, link arms with your comrades, black and white, standing as one. Then take this hope and healing into your family's garden, local allotments, and open spaces in the public domain. Take it on holiday abroad, plant it there. Spread the war of love. Even just one seed at a time. Start there.

CHAPTER 16

Migrating Goose

Just wait. Just allow yourselves, and others, to weep.

Good morning, robin bird, oh how I love you, I really do. I wish you would let me hug you before you fly away. Or even allow me to stroke your majestic red breast. Your singing is so sweet, robin bird, but I need you to be quiet. "Ssh, ssh, birdy, I hear squawking." Gazing out of my snow globe window I see flying geese, it is not really the sweetest of sounds, yet it is irresistible to listen to their honk, honk, honk.

They are flying off to hotter climates. I wonder is the honking not just them communicating a "Come on boys," encouragement, or "You're going the wrong way, Goose". No, aside from that, I wonder is it a sound almost akin to the cries of a mother in labour – a painful, yet joy-accompanied cry? Many geese know the harsh treacherous migration that awaits, they have taken this route many times before. They know the reality of fatigued wings and the weeping eyes from the harsh winds to come. They know what it is like to bury comrades who did not quite make it. Yet many know the joy of arriving safely and escaping winter. Even though this is what they need to do, I ponder do they cry out as there is a grief attached to this move? Do they really want to leave?

Can you imagine the scene, a crowed picnic table

with geese chattering about their memories of adventurous day trips? Can you see the geese wearing backpacks and clutching their wicker picnic hampers in the Lake District? I see them basking in the sunshine and toasting to the celebration of time together on treasured soil. I am not sure that their taste buds appreciate the left-over bottle of prosecco discovered on the yacht. I bet they have tried a tipple or two, if not the cool, crisp soft Cumbrian water, in a crystal cut glass, would equally suffice for the occasion. There is mourning attached to all loss, surely this too applies to the goose?

My Auntie Annie once told me that geese do not leave the side of the injured; maybe that's where humans have gone wrong, we are not often very willing to often stay, to wait for healing – we are impatient and inhumane. Grief leave from work is very limited and does not even exist for the true grief found in infertility and betrayal amongst other losses in this life.

Mourning is a process and it takes time, it is not allowed time. It is restricted. My guess is that rather than pain fulfilling its necessary cycle, the body instead concludes that part of oneself must die instead in order to continue to perform. Do you not see the economic, health and social disaster here? Starve the employee of grieving leave and instead bring back an employee who has died in places. This world is too cruel; this is not how it should be.

People are wounded by grief and need loved back to operating at full capacity; more importantly they

Migrating Goose

need loved back to life. If the Church fails to do that, which it often does, then I call upon legal change for grief leave. Let us cover the mourning, like the mother who has just miscarried, with a blanket of love, and discontinue the feeding of death in hearts across this nation. Be like the goose, just stay by the side of the injured, just stop. Just wait, just allow yourselves and others to weep. I repeat, just wait, just allow yourselves and others to weep.

*

The time has come for me to migrate to England and alone; I see myself as a goose I'm having to leave Northern Ireland, I sense a deep calling into the teaching profession. Yet simultaneously I need to leave for my emotional survival. I can no longer withstand the bitterness. I feel a deep calling like the geese, a natural stirring that I try to ignore. What about my gaggle? A gaggle I hear you say, yes, a group of geese is known as a gaggle. My gaggle is a group of my dear friends from when I was a very little one. I do not want to leave them. Yet, as bonded as we are, they too have their own callings to relocate, to marry and have children. I realise I cannot pursue these same goals, let me rephrase that in absolute undiluted honesty. I am unable to follow that path, I can have friends outside my gaggle but those relationships are dysfunctional. I place disproportionate demands on women to fulfil my void. With men I fear deep intimacy and can almost discard boyfriends without a care. I am aware that I need to mend those parts of me that are shredded, vacant and hurting.

I do not have the skills to marry or commit because of my past. I know this, but I do not vocalise this pain to anyone. Instead, I pretend the choices I make are deliberate, but I have no choice, I am unable to make intimate healthy attachments, romantically and sometimes even relationally, this causes devastation. I have fledged the nest, many years ago, but now I need to fledge the nest of Northern Ireland. I am going to build with my hands a comfy nest in England. I only have an old sewing box full of scrap material and broken threads. I am creative though, so I am confident this will suffice. I am aware that this thinking is idealistic. Deep down, I know migrating will not stop the pain. I no longer live with Hands. Yet her legacy lives in me. I am a refugee in search of a "Home". I have a house, but I need a "Home". I suspect I will continue to spend hours in my car driving; to avoid opening the front door of my pain trigger. That door reminds me that in my heart I am homeless. Christmas triggers a panic. "What if friends forget to invite me?", "What if the turkey is too small this year?" I rely on the open doors of others, as my family does not welcome me. Driving seems to distract me. It makes me feel hopeful that one day I will stumble across "Home". For now I'm lost. Very lost and have no compass, only my faith. I really want to say sorry. I am sorry to anyone who has suffered for this. I continue to utter another line of the Lord's Prayer, "Father, forgive us our trespasses."

I wish I could mend these places broken in me, but I do not know how. So, I guess I conclude subconsciously that if these areas are broken in me relationally then I will excel elsewhere instead. I am sorry to anyone who fell victim to my quest for belonging. I wonder in this revealed moment are many of the world's hurts caused by this same desire? To feel love and belong? I am curious to know are all hurtful actions propelled by this force? Maybe that is what happened to Hands, the hurt I inflicted on others was not physical, but it was inconsiderate.

Oh, how I wish my snow globe could be bubble-wrapped and left alone. I feel a sudden move a shake, it feels like an earthquake. I am now a migrating goose, aged 27 and I am moving to England, alone. Geese migrate together and take turns to lead each other in the V formation. I am alone. I mourn my home already, just as I imagine the geese must mourn theirs. After all, grief is not limited to physical death, the loss of anything can cause grief. I am certain that geese miss foraging for food at their local geese restaurants. I am sure they mourn saying goodbye to the leaves and twigs that they carefully selected after watching home-improvement programmes through living room windows. Do not tell me that geese do not cry when they have to leave a ready-made bird estuary gifted to them. I am certain they recall the fond memories of brew making as they awaited the estate agents to sign.

Little One's Whisper

Now they are called to leave they weep. I feel they weep, and often, as they say goodbye to the comfort in the familiar. Alongside the weeping, I am sure there is excitement too. A new beginning. Space away from painful memories. An escape.

I am alone in a new land and far from home. My visits to Annie grew less and less as I grew up, this was due to a mixture of geographical distance, my shame of who I had now become and my disabling emotional wounds. I self-diagnose, perhaps I am slightly homesick as I have just arrived in England. I get dressed in an attempt to distract myself from my emotional pain. I select my clothes – an unusual choice: black sunglasses, black trousers, a black jumper, a black knee-length coat and black Converse trainers. Not one splash of colour. Perhaps I am simply missing my Irish coffee haunts. My phone rings and the announcement made; Annie is dead. My guilt rises, oh Annie, I did not visit you towards the end. My mind absorbs the hospital smell, the noises of machines, the isolation for her in her failing body. I cry louder than the geese. I scream, "no Annie please come back, there is something I need to tell you yet." As I know very well death is final, it does not offer the chance for that last hug, conversation or the opportunity to offer deep gratitude. No, death is final, learn from my mistake and keep loved ones informed regularly of your affection towards them.

I decide not to fly home for the funeral, I feel like a disloyal imposter, instead I pick up a sympathy card and pen these words. 'Annie, my Annie, oh how I wish you knew how my love for you grew and grew, as time went by and I grew up. I realised all the sacrifices you made to bring me up, you got weaker as I got bigger. Hands and Dad visited less, but I've no excuse since I have passed my driving test. I failed you, Annie, I want you to know. I let the poison of my household life convince me that you, too, wanted me out of sight. How very wrong of me I must confess, as I know the woollen craft I made for you never left your dressing table. Our bond never stopped, the love never died. I see now that today I arose with grief inside my heart. In choosing my clothes of black you whispered to my soul: it is my time to depart. Annie, please, know how often I praised you by name, no one will ever love me quite the same. I found a birthday card you wrote to me when I was eight, it says love, always underlined, with £50 enclosed inside. Now, as an adult, that card reads, here is a huge chunk of my pension and all of my heart. I can imagine my aunt Annie from heaven saying, "sweetheart, my love for you was my life's delight." You, my Annie, will always be loved so much. I hope one day I grow up to be more like you in all I do. As your love was so pure, generous and true. PS I miss laughing with you.'

*

For a long time, my new-found career in teaching saved me. I had the geographical space and time that I needed to rebuild a new nest. I was happy despite missing my gaggle. Personally, I grew. I learnt to form healthy attachments outside my gaggle. One family in particular the Burfitts invited me into their nest as their own non-blood bird. I lived in their home for many years. Janet, the mum of grown-up girls who had all married, except the youngest goose. So, Janet, young goose and I lived together for quite some time. For the first time in my life since my dad remarried, I felt so loved within a family nest. This family are so special and I know I was divinely appointed to meet them.

They too have their own grief story as Janet's husband Malcom, the father of her three daughters, was killed tragically in a road traffic accident. Leaving behind a huge void in their nest; the youngest goose was only four years old. Tragedy had already struck their lives as Janet's mother, Janet and her girls had a horrific car accident themselves. It left them too injured in hospital to attend Janet's mother's funeral who had been killed instantly in the car crash. Janet refused as the mother goose of this family to allow tragedy to define her. Janet's steadfast faith in Christ and her relentless pursuit of his presence was, and will always be, an inspiration to me. She passed this beautiful gift onto her three daughters and all of them have shown me in real, tangible ways the love of God shared over supper in their homes and gardens.

They unofficially adopted me into aspects of their family. Words fail to express the depth of gratitude and love that I will always have for each member of this family. Under the cover of a loving home, I flourished too. Within a year of teaching RE, I was promoted to head of department. For a decade that department went from strength to strength. Despite being adopted and successful I still had wounds that bled. After all, as kind as this family were, I was and am not family, and as successful as I became in my job, I still felt like a failure to my own family. I still have wounds that needed healing. Skin cannot fix skin. Some of my wounds I was too scared to share. How can I say I was unable to marry? That I feared my husband would be violent towards me because my skin had been damaged as a child. How could I admit to my peers that I struggle with intimacy?

Deep down I felt unworthy of love, I had attachment issues, I became a workaholic to hide from my pain. I hurt friends and dropped boyfriends in a cold-hearted way. Unhealthy patterns stitch to me like a seamstress diligently sewing a patchwork quilt. It requires such labour, that does not deter me. I am, after all, in sole pursuit on performance-based acceptance and the sheer determination to hide my attachment difficulties. Subconsciously my mind selects the fabric, the thread and the materials. I sit down at this imaginary sewing machine to create a "new me." I am going to be loved. So, I choose the patterns, work-aholism, addiction to nicotine, escapism, OCD rituals to make me feel safe and hiding behind the mask of my natural extrovert personality at times. While at other times I isolated myself from my peers to avoid conversations targeted toward me about marriage or commitment. I sit at this imaginary sewing machine and do overtime. The thing is, my sewing machine is running out of charge. I am finding it harder and harder to numb my pain. Yet I carry on, until I have no more thread and all that consists of me is a broken body which is no longer fit for purpose.

To make matters worse, the doctors think I am going to lose my womb, I already had womb surgery to remove fibroids, but they are growing back at lightning speed. They cut me open. Like a C-section. They injected me with steroids too. I feel so ill. I keep working; I have gained three stone. I sense in time my womb will be seized from my body, the doctors to suspect so. But my heart knows it has begun to slowly say goodbye to my womb every day. A daily death of the hope of motherhood ever being reality for me. Everything inside me is broken, so I turn to Christian counselling. Today I met a woman who heard my story she looked disinterested and disbelieving, she went into a drawer and selected a tatty piece of ripped paper and a cheap Biro pen and she wrote '12pm appointment referred' with a number for me to call a referral. How can I find the strength to pick up the phone and source more help? Is this the sum of me? A scrap piece of paper? So I decide to end this mess by taking my own life. I do not want to die, but I cannot live in this body. I want to silence this pain in a dirty lake, I do not want to pollute the ocean with my filth. So, I stand by the lake, I see my reflection through littered rubbish, skimmed in oil, I do not see a single glimmer of hope, I am undone. There is nothing left of me except this breath in my lungs.

I use this breath to cry out to God, and he rushes an old hymn to the forefront of my mind, *It is Well with My Soul* by Horatio Spafford. Sadly, it is not well with my soul, but I wonder if God cares enough to come to my rescue yet again. Alma, I am so sorry that I let you get ill. I tried to nourish you, but if the truth be told I never fully appreciated your worth. I need God to restore you. Everything else was more important that you. I am so sorry Alma, time and time again I cause you to bleed and still you remain my loyal friend, leading my lost life to Christ without tiring. I need to make time to allow you to rest, reflect and replenish without me constantly forcing you to work overtime. Interestingly, I never go to bed without charging my mobile phone. I take the time to plug it into the charger and caress it into sleep mode. Yet, with you Alma, I have an unrealistic expectation that you can run on empty. I am sorry. Only God knows what I truly need to restore my soul.

I come to my God in prayer. I get back into my car and I pray that God will lead me to the right help. On my third attempt I find Anne. I sense she is different, there is no mention of God on her website but when I met her, I feel God in the room. I see him in her brown eyes. God did not leave me at the lake. He guided my steps with butterfly sightings until I safely landed at Anne's door. I feel I know this counsellor somehow, but I don't, I guess what I recognise in her is "Annie Love".

I go on to test Anne's ability to handle my pain. She

must pass my tests; I reject her like I have been rejected. I shout, I am silent and speak only to criticise her therapy in a desperate attempt to force her to reject me. She refuses, one day she interrupts the silence and says to me, "why don't you write to your inner child?" Little did she know that for six months prior to this meeting, I had tried to unlock my trauma through writing. I could not do it, I tried to make it academic. The book that Anne saw inside me could not be more different – it is simply a raw, unrehearsed and unchanged collection of words. Quite simply it is just therapy. Perhaps at different stages in all our lives, you too need the space, the blank paper, the removal of position and the time to be a child again and simply admit you hurt and need help to mend your broken soul. This patchwork quilt looks so successful in places, but to what cost?

*

I carry on until my womb is taken from my body, with the help of an epidural and a C-section (abdominal hysterectomy). As I was being put to sleep, I hummed the song from the lake where I wanted to die, "it is well with my soul" until the oxygen mask muffled the sound, in that moment my nurse – obviously a Christian – continued the humming for me. God was in that room and was permitting my infertility. Her Alma communicating to my Alma. Not in words, not in a discussion. Rather she simply allowed her Alma to hold my hand and hum. I am a goose alone and far from home. I cried tears I have never heard before. My fibroid

Migrating Goose

was now the size of a 10lb baby. They could not operate via keyhole. My tears fall onto goose-feathered pillows. I hide under the pillow as the sound is too harrowing for even me. How can I be infertile in a fertile world? I must harness this pain. I must accept my outcome as my reality. I cannot bear my own children and I too accept I cannot continue in my job which will deny me nurturing other people's children too, so I resign. My body and mind needs time. This loss was huge. Yet it had instant ramifications for me. I had to say goodbye to my beautiful rented home that I had papered and it appeared to everyone that I had finally created a "Home". It wasn't mine. It was pretty but fake advertising on my part.

Still I said goodbye to it. Losing my salary only afforded me the funds to rent a room and take "time out" to finish this book. I kissed my bed goodbye.

Aside from the basics everything was taken by charity, even sentimental treasures. My snowglobe is so tight. I'm sectioned to a room within it. All the while my peers look at me like I am mad. I simply obeyed the call of God to free Little One. Yet, I ache all over.

God, I hate my life, how could you allow this to be in my story, with barely any time given to digest my future? A pregnant friend rings hoping for my excitement. But all I can offer her is anger; I see my ex-pupils in uniform walking home, the pain and grief hits again. I want to cut off this fertile world from my life. I am angry with sprouting flowers, singing birds and the season of spring shouting in my face. Leave me, leave me to wilt. I weep again, this time I weep at how bitter I have become. I cannot allow this bitterness to take root. I know I must absorb my hurts like a sponge and hang them on the line to dry in the spring air.

I suspect part of me will always be aware of this void, but I cannot let it dominate my future. Annie was a mother without her own biological children. I too can be just that. So, I buy flowers for myself and write cards. Formally and ceremonially, I say goodbye to the parts of me no longer destined to be. I cut them loose from my Alma and cling onto Sofia. Guide me in wisdom to find a way to cohabit with this pain. We as a society do not honour losses aside from death in a formal way. I think we should, I think there is a need to plan a funeral for the loss of health, hopes, jobs and relationships. Even if that loss was not taken in death it died to you and me. Oh, I see the death of a dream held as tenderly as a newborn and nursed into a hopeful place in our souls as a deep loss. We do not allow ourselves a wake. Rather life marches on.

So today I hold my own funeral for the death of everything I have lost. I begin my grief procession imaging the comfort of being on my mother's knee. Being held in her unconditional love. I end my grief procession in the sanitary aisle. Saying goodbye to the menstrating women I was. I let the darkness consume me as only in doing so can I ever radiate light again. I may never understand the purpose of this pain here on earth, but I trust that God will tell me in heaven. I surrender my body for you my God for a deep clean. Help me to grieve, help me to let go of the hurt as it returns in different seasons

Migrating Goose

and stages of my life. Provide for me a bridge my God between the fertile and infertile world as I trust you to create new fertility in the soul of my destiny. For now, I am a goose alone in England after a long 14 years and counting. My heart longs to go home; be with me and beside me as my nest here is shaking. I trust in you to show me the right time to fly away. Surely it is time to migrate back home soon, or maybe go to Spain? I would accept anything other than looking through this glass pane. Surely my winter is melting away and summer is coming to greet me. I suspect I am grounded here until I finish my quest in publishing my book.

I do not know how you know where to go dear geese? I can only imagine that you trust your instinct and are travelling by faith. You hover over the waters, smelling your way to safer routes. I suspect you take advice from the older birds too. Those who have gone before.

However, you travel, you stick together in your infamous V formation. You are an inspiration to our failing social stuctrures in the U.K.

I salute you precious geese for your bravery and humility. No one buys tickets to view your majestic choreographed flying migration performance. I wonder are you honking for our attention? Calling upon us to look up, chat less and take inspiration from God's creation.

Safe travels dear geese. Thank-you for your wisdom and example. PS, please refrain from honking after 11 p.m. In return I will refrain from buying goose feather pillows from now on.

CHAPTER 17

Dolly

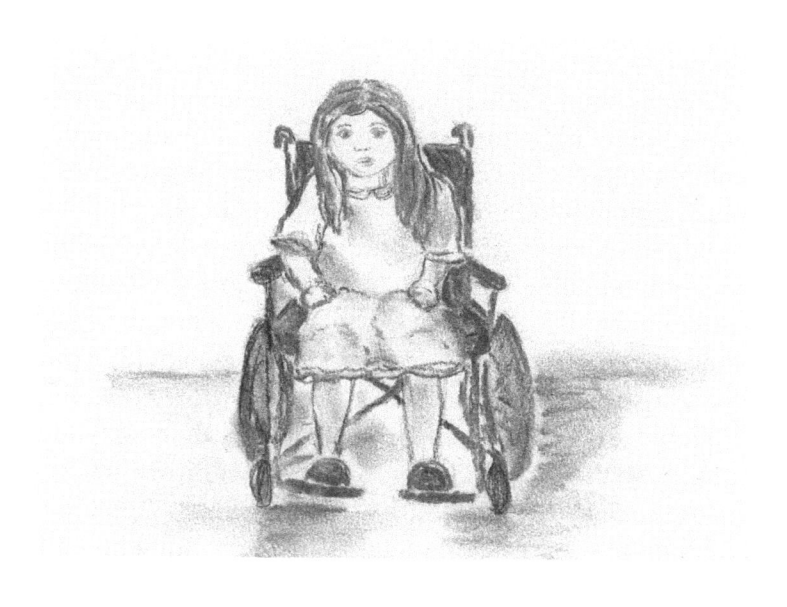

That is what we do when we mishandle people. We bury them prematurely into a destiny they were never born to fulfil.

Time. I wish this time never had to arrive. This time has always been there from the beginning. It simply had to wait inside, not in complete silence though. Rather I felt and heard this pain beating like a swinging pendulum back and forth, tick-tock, loudly beating each count on the hour of the clock. I think this pain eagerly awaited the time I committed its voice to paper. It existed in the dark corridors of my mind; it flooded my heart so many times I had to crawl into bed in the foetal position to drain the tears of flooding that required release. Yet, the full exposure of this pain had to arise at the right time. I do not know how the pain knew the seconds or minutes of its outpouring. I guess it intuitively knew, like the unborn child choosing its moment to descend down the birth canal. I am not the only one in a snow globe. Dolly lives in hers too. Locked away and far out of sight. I hope to change this, with all my might! Shake, shake, shake. Snow, snow, snow.

To open this wound before would have prevented Little One from voicing her own needs and pain. This pain of Dolly was of course integrated into my heart, but I had to sieve it out of my soul, seal it at large in a Tupperware container in the pantry of my mind until I had dealt with my trauma.

Little One's Whisper

My motivation to carry on lifting my pen was driven by my unquenchable love for Dolly. My desire to see her find emotional and spiritual freedom is paramount. My passion to stop at nothing until I can secure a haven for her is in my DNA, but still I had to wait. It is like Dolly too has her own unique inner clock synchronised to mine despite being separated by the Irish Sea. Yet we beat our clocks together and in time. It is almost as though our pendulums communicate deeply and often even without words, touch, or direct knowledge, no, rather there is a deep knowing. Her pain is my pain, her hurt is my hurt and her life matters to me more than any other. It is a bond that I imagine exists between a mother and her daughter. In the absence of my mother, Dolly is like my own somehow. She isn't simply a sister, but a soul for whom I would sacrifice my own life to ease her suffering, even momentarily. I named my sister Dolly, my wide-eyed, dark eyebrowed beautiful sister with a button nose. I certainly did not inherit that gene. I joke that my nose is so sharp that it could warrant its own postcode, like a mountainous landscape that pushes my facial structure to the next county.

I know it is an exaggeration, but I love my sister's cute nose. It is so sweet. Some faces are like that, aren't they? They almost require us to tiptoe gently around their face, like any drastic movement could tarnish their serene beauty. I repeat that my mission has always been to help her. Despite the fact that I have not committed her to ink does not mean I have not carried her on my back. I have always enjoyed piggyback rides,

Dolly

but this childish game has caused my back to break as the years have passed.

I wasn't designed, nor is anyone designed to carry someone else in this life. Not even full-time carers, yet in this broken care system that is quite often the sad reality facing many. Full-time carers are offered pennies for their service. They do not receive a living wage or a pension. I would go as far as to say government policies take direct advantage of families caring for their loved ones. The wife desperate to keep her disabled husband at home for his holistic well-being is taken advantage of due to her self-sacrifice. This needs to change.

My Dolly is poorly. I do not care for her 24/7, but even with her care package I am left with a short-fall. Her limited financial support barely covers basic needs never mind the luxuries afforded to those in society who are well. I did not notice that I learned to ride a bike before Dolly even though she is slightly older than me by just a year. I didn't notice she showed signs of being different. Why would I notice? I just accepted her.

I employed her on an exchange of sweets basis to make pretend radio stations with me, of course I was the DJ. But she selected the single vinyl records that we bought with our pocket money. It was not a slick show but oh how I wish I had kept those cassette tapes. As time went on Dolly's cognitive difficulties became more pronounced, yet she received mainstream schooling. She amazed me; she amazes me. Despite her struggles she beat me at Connect Four and Battleships. Being the youngest I found it hard not to win without an extreme outward explosion. The funny thing is, I wish now she had won over me in this life.

So many times, I wish it was me and not her who had her legs fail her. Somehow it is harder to watch the suffering of a loved one; I do not think you watch it – that is too remote and distant. It is like the illness of a loved one is contagious. You do not enjoy your faculties the same, you resent your working body, somehow you're scared to show it working at full capacity and somehow diminish non-disabled living into a mere nothing. Simple things like saying I had a walk today can act as a painful, cutting electric knife, gnawing through the tough meat of disability. You see no longer was it just mental, physically my Dolly was breaking slowly. If I could describe my sister's mental difficulties, I would describe a beautiful car with talented wheels, but instead of four wheels there are three. As time went on people began to focus on the missing wheel, yet not me. She taught me from her unique gifts and intellect that her three wheels were somehow better than my four.

There is a vulnerability to Dolly, that I accept, she is now classified as a vulnerable adult and disabled. Although she has rightly embraced the new buzz term 'differently abled'. Society treats those who are vulnerable as inferior all too often. How dare they! Everyone is uniquely gifted both mentally and physically; there is no greater vulnerability or disability that exists in the lives in those who think they are above it themselves. Oh, that moment awaits us all. In times of failing health

Dolly

and in the disabled suspension of healthy living when depression and fear arrests the heart into a prison of silence. Perhaps some are unable to seek professional intervention out of the worry of being labelled weak. Everyone, and I repeat everyone, should be prescribed counselling throughout their lives as freely as a pharmacist prescribes paracetamol for headaches. The trauma in this life can often be more painful than a migraine and demands appropriate action.

As Dolly and I grew up, I became her spare wheel, adapting unknowingly my language, my approach and love. We fought. We fight. Of course we do, we are sisters and could not be more physically, emotionally or characteristically different. Yet our bond is deep and our pendulums beat together. My sister and I ran and played. Her legs worked until she was 17 then slowly her foot began to drag, and she needed lots of tests. I recall the day I saw her wheelchair in the garage which then was not needed often. In that moment my inner world was in total ruins. No one asked me how I felt, but if I was to describe that day, I would say it was as frightening as the day I watched the Twin Towers collapse. I know nothing I could do could rebuild the past. The doctors never fully uncovered the cause, suffice to say it appeared like MS, although the exact condition remains a mystery. My dad cried and it broke him too, but the dysfunction in the family unit was not secure enough to bring unity. This moment in time simply signalled a deeper turning of division and isolation. I wanted to revisit the peace talks from 'Raw

War', but I knew it was futile. So, I surrendered regrettably into allowing Dolly to be handled by them.

My Dolly, my porcelain Dolly. I do not want this doctor's report for you. I wish I could lift you onto my bedroom shelf like the porcelain doll I have there. I hate dolls but a relative bought me an expensive porcelain doll and, out of monetary respect, I have never binned her. This doll has blonde curly hair and a black velvet dress trimmed in lace. She is wearing patent shoes and holds a tiny wooden violin. She is supported to stand upright by an invisible metal rod up her back. I remember staring at her, never quite understanding that she was not real. Oh, how I wish I could pull that metal rod and fix it upon my sister's back both in terms of her illness, but also in an attempt to allow the emotional changes of those close to her to act as such a support. Instead, I knew, like many times before this capacity for change was not going to occur no matter how hard I tried.

Dolly is like a porcelain doll. Despite porcelain being very resistant against chips and cracks to its surface, handled wrongly the cracks will appear. I smashed my porcelain doll that day. I didn't have to throw her against a wall. I simply removed her supportive back rod and let her fall onto my wooden dressing table. She received fatal head injuries. So I buried her in the bin in her fine clothes and tucked her violin under her arm. That is what we do when we mishandle people, we bury them prematurely into a destiny they were never born to fulfil.

Dolly

My sister Dolly this is your hour, stop the clocks, stop the hours, the minutes and seconds of your racing mind. Just stop. Do not listen with one eye on your phone, scrolling through empty messages on Facebook. Dolly, you deserve clocks to be stopped, so does every real-life doll when they unleash their pain. Please, listen to Dolly through me. I hope my Dolly, I do you justice and one day you are given the opportunity to release this pain yourself. I've tried to give you that voice, but I was met with opposition. So, for now I will do it on your behalf. I tried to get social services to help give Dolly more help. They think I'm interfering. Really? I hope no family member of theirs ever finds themselves in this place. She is my blood, to them she is a user. What a degrading term used by social services: 'a service user'. I am sure this term was selected as it was deemed more empowering than a patient or a client. Still, I challenge it. The very title strips the humanity out of the human in need. Anyone requiring social services support is unique, they have a soul and should be referred to by name. Preferably an honorary title before, such as Mr, Mrs or Ms. These individuals may be accessing services, but they are not users. They are simply in need, aren't we all in some way or another?

Christian counsellors too failed Dolly, one saying she did not have the skills to handle her unique character. So, this counsellor and social services forced me to be Dolly's everything even though it was killing me. Christian counselling services, perhaps counselling services in general, need reform alongside social services. It is not good enough and I am not scared to admit that, not to criticize but to demand reform.

Life took me away to England, but my devotion to Dolly saw me return each school holiday to take her on holiday. Then she was based at home. I thought it was safe as I assumed, wrongly, that Hands' explosive attacks had stopped fully once I had left. I had largely bore the brunt of Hands; Dolly had not been immune, but never did I suspect that she would hurt her in her failing body. I was wrong; I should have done more. I should never have left Northern Ireland. Alongside my regret is the reality that, if I had stayed, I would have died fully inside and been no support to Dolly whatsoever. Still, I carry regret.

I returned from England one summer holiday when Dolly, who was still largely mobile although weak and in more and more need of a wheelchair, said to me that Hands gave her a black eye. I had to leave my sister in the jacuzzi of the hotel. She was so tiny, so frail, a kind pool attendant said they would keep their eye on her. I had no choice, I had to go to the changing room toilets to vomit. I did not know what to do. I was lost in the pain of my Dolly.

That night, as I was assisting Dolly into bed, she broke. It was like the shards of her porcelain body and mind could not keep it together any more. She simply shattered into pieces. First came the shouting and rage, then the uncontrollable sobbing. Then the direct anger at me for leaving her. I understood all her emotions and I too was in pain. I suggested a drink from the mini-bar.

Dolly

It was declined. I offered to go out and get Northern Irish ice cream named Pooh Bear, which I would argue is the best I have ever tasted. Still, this was declined. So, in desperation I rang my dad to explain the situation. I do not know what I expected from him, and he had largely been emotionally absent. Yet, I was hopeful that in this moment of crisis that he would intervene. He listened at first, but I heard Hands laughing as she entertained friends in their home. His tone then changed and he said, "I am pulling out the landline plug and turning off my mobile. You are interrupting our evening of pleasure." "Pleasure" I exclaimed, "how dare you utter those words." The phone went dead.

My mind momentarily flashed back to one evening when I was about 16. I had returned home from an ice-skating disco. My dad physically assaulted me. For the first and thankfully last time. I suspect he assumed I had been sleeping with my boyfriend. I had not. Yet, I think he wanted to warn me of the consequences if I did. Dolly woke up due to me screaming, even though my dad had my face smothered with a cushion. Hands then came rushing down the stairs to say, "you have woken Dolly." I assumed at first, she was directing this to my dad. Rather, she was directing that to me. I do not know why I keep trying to relate, to reach for their help. It is a very bleak dynamic.

So, I find myself alone with my broken porcelain doll in our hotel room. I crawl into her bed beside her and mould myself into her foetus position and slowly begin to rock her. Rocking a child to sleep conjures up romantic images of open fires and mothers cradling their newborn on a rocking chair. My Dolly is not a child, but a vulnerable adult, she does not fit into my arms. Yet my intuition tells me that there is still comfort for an adult to be rocked. Otherwise hammocks would have no retail value. I rock her, whispering edifying words into her life. I wipe away her tears as I silence my own. "It will be OK Dolly, I promise." I will try my best to break this snow globe for you.

Nothing I ever did before stopped Hands. Yet to hurt a vulnerable adult was the lowest of all her assaults. Returning from the trip I helped Dolly securely to her room. Grabbing Hands and shoving her against the wall while my dad rushed to Hands' protection, I screamed, "I do not come to this house because of this. Hurt her again and the police will be at your door."

I did not ring the police there and then as I was too scared of them from my own childhood, too scared they would make me out to be a liar. Dad said, "oh it was just a one-off carer-stress incident and Dolly provoked it." Nothing provokes violence. Dolly had found a voice and I suspect her crime was using it for the first time. Dolly was scared she had nowhere else to go, nor did I. I could not fix this for her, but I just hoped that I'd done enough to stop it happening again. It did not stop it happening again. I received a phone call to say Dolly had had enough. She was at her craft group and got the leader to ring social services. Hands had tried to choke her with damp clothes that she cruelly shoved in her face when she was in bed. As if that is not horrifying enough, Dolly did

Dolly

not have the strength to stop the attack and all the while she screamed, "Why take these off the dryer when they are damp, you lazy careless bitch."

It was Easter and I was coming home as it was in keeping with the school holidays. Never could I expose this at work, although do not teachers suffer domestic abuse and family breakdowns? There needs to be greater compassion shown towards the profession and the opportunity for teachers to take leave of absence outside the structured set school holidays. My experience here has shown me there is an expectation to pretend all is well. Yet we live in a broken society and I am sure others suffer this reality within the profession. I arrive to find my sister in a nursing home. A nursing home? Yes, due to her need for a care package the emergency placement found her there. Two of my gaggle accompanied me to visit her there. I promised Dolly I would get her out, she collapsed in my arms and made the noises of a wounded animal, so too did I, inside. But I had to be strong, this was not my time to crumble. Little did I know then that I needed to be strong for over a decade to come.

Looking at her beautiful face I said, "I am coming to take you out for lunch tomorrow." At this stage my sister could weight-bear and I could help her into my car and fold her wheelchair away. The next morning, I demanded a meeting with social services. Of all the places that this meeting could have been held it was scheduled to be in a cold room, in a derelict mental hospital. It says it all, cold and indifferent. Dad was nowhere to be found so I went alone into that icy cold room, to be met by four women protesting that they had done all they could to prevent this outcome. In the end I said you have 48 hours to find my sister a placement. It was found and I took Dolly to Ikea to kit her out with basic furniture, rugs, lights and blankets. At least this way her bedroom was not institutionalised, I wanted more than Ikea, but it was all I could afford. Her new placement had a hydro-pool and people her age. She could work part time, attend church and activities. It was brought to light that Hands had stopped her evening activities for her convenience and forced her to bed by 6pm. This was neglect and my dad did not stop it.

This placement was not perfect, but it was, without a shadow of a doubt, an upgraded snow globe. It has been where she has lived for a decade now. I continued teaching and it worked well as the school holidays were free to continue to give her as many holidays away as I could to hotels and spas, and I even found a disabled hotel abroad – we made it work. Every spare penny I had was spent making things better for Dolly. Latterly Dolly's condition has worsened, she now uses an electric wheelchair full time. She needs help with personal care, overhead hoists to transfer her to her chair, a shower or bed, and an adapted vehicle. Her medication has caused weight gain and all of this combined made my holiday efforts so much harder. I had to find help. Now only one place in Northern

Dolly

Ireland could facilitate our holidays as it was the only B&B with overhead ceiling and shower hoist required for moving and handling Dolly.

I tried to get carers' help, but people kept letting me down, so I forced myself to do the job of two men alone even on Christmas Day. I eventually found a lovely lady that helped at a cost; she has become a dear friend and support and has been there for us both ever since. Dolly adores her, she doesn't care about a uniform and she doesn't wear gloves, she says, "that is what a washing machine and soap are for." She sees the human above the disability.

She arrived early one morning to assist me to shower Dolly and she said, "Excuse my shoes I wear these for showering." It was so early I had not yet brewed my morning coffee and I retorted, "Oh my goodness, I have never met someone who showers in shoes before," in that moment we laughed and bonded instantly. She said, "No, I do not wear shoes for showering, I wear shoes to assist showering." Before she left that morning, she said to me, "You should write a book," I said "What, a book about my gullible anecdotes?" and she said, "No, a book about your life, and Dolly's life."

Quite often God uses others to nudge us into the next arena of our destiny. I have often found he uses non-Christians too. After all, their souls belong to God whether they believe in him or not. Alma's speak regardless to other Almas.

*

My failing health made it increasingly difficult to find the mental, spiritual and emotional energy required for Dolly. She sensed that I was slightly less involved and often verbally attacked me in her frustration. Covid descent compounded this. We manage on zoom, but writing this book became harder as I was not present for Dolly. My Dolly is not perfect and nor am I, I lack patience at times. But the one thing we both agree on is that Dolly needs her own home. I have written this book in the hope to purchase that for her one day. I hope this home can be big enough to home others too. I hope one day this book can help change the Disability Act in Northern Ireland to ensure the sub-standard facilities available are exposed and more is done for other Dolly's in need. It is almost impossible to source a disabled hire car in N.I. direct from an airport. I am determined to change this. I also wrote this book as my back is too sore to carry this for much longer. I need to find Dolly a home and fast. Our pendulums need to stop and simply be free to beat in unity as sisters. Not two sisters beating for survival. A song from Les Misérables performed by Mark McMullen from Northeren Ireland springs to mind; I will change the masculine to the feminine in my mind thinking of the song, "Bring Him Home." Please play and protest to God on her behalf.

Tick-tock, tick-tock, I am waiting on you my saviour to stop this clock. Back and forth, day and night until the time your power is light. Light that moves for all to see, the God of love is powering me. I bow my head and say another section of the Lord's Prayer, "Forgive those who trespass against us."

It is difficult to forgive that which should never be with no apology offered, yet I know for our ultimate release from pain, that this is now the path we must embark on together. I am not sure if forgiveness means reconciled relationships. Trust is required for that, honesty and change. I fear if my dad or Hands read this book that it would simply invite more trouble. I will not live in fear any more though. I take Dolly's hand and we take our first moments together into the future. Her on her wheels and me on my feet. Dolly translates exactly the same in the Spanish language. I am not surprised, no one is closer to my soul than my Spanish Dolly.

The time is coming for Dolly and I to reunite now we have our vaccinations. Her care home and the care given to her there by the lovely girls has been our lifeline.

Yet, Dolly requires more than a "lifeline." She simply needs full deliverance from her snowglobe. She needs counselling, and an oprn fire and dreams fulfilled.

My Dolly, My Spanish Doll. I wrote this for you. Others had to wait to hear your story, but I opened the Tupperware box I kept in my mind containing your story everyday.

I will never stop fighting for your freedom. Never, Snow, Snow, Snow, Shake, Shake Shake. Spring is getting ready for this glass dome to break. My love for you is overcoming Winter, with God fighting for us both!

CHAPTER 18

Rebirth

I thought at times that writing was difficult. I was wrong. What pains me the most now, is letting go of the secrets that were once unwritten.

Shake, shake, shake. Snow, snow, snow. I fasten my red shoes gifted to me by my adult body in chapter one. They are red patent and beautiful. They have stretched to a UK size five and fit my feet perfectly. Yet, if the truth be told, the grips on the sole have little traction. So, I use some sandpaper on the sole to try to wear them in. A few grooves have appeared, I could never wear them before without slipping, as the ground underfoot was always covered in a blanket of snow.

I feel a thaw in the air. I see slush. Still, I am hesitant. It is difficult to forecast the weather. Weather specialists even struggle. Only God knows, he holds the future in his hands.

Still, I am scared. Standing to my feet, I slip and slide I am very nervous, quite honestly I could do with ordering a pair of Dr Martens. I remember my cherry red pair. They gripped snow and ice and kept my naturally icy feet that little bit warmer! My red shoes do not have this same comfort. Yet I trust the shoes I have been gifted are fit for purpose. I hope the snow will stop, or God will give me the ability to cover snow-covered pavements with new-found confidence and security.

Oh, how I wish I could tie my words into a literary bow and conclude in a seamless conclusion. I cannot, I have not been miraculously delivered from my snow globe by angelic hosts. Storybook resolutions seldom happen in real life. I cannot even name this final chapter my conclusion. It is simply the beginning – my rebirth. God still did the miraculous in my life though. The miracle is that I found the strength to finish this book despite being covered by bruises and cuts from the intensity of this last push. Like the marks left of a newborn from the use of metal stirrups used to assist in the delivery.

*

My childminder, my friend, my biggest fan, suddenly and unexpectantly died. The Irish Sea and Covid-19 restrictions meant that I could not be at 'home' and present at her funeral. I was alone in my sorrow aside from the comfort of a few friends. She had spent her last weeks on this earth in an ICU ward. I prayed earnestly that her dry bones and failing organs would come alive once more and they would throw off the ventilators and machines in full health and conscious strength.

I trusted God fully for her healing and breakthrough. Like many times in my life, I had to accept that the sovereignty of God had other plans in store for her body. God was calling her home. I was pulling her back with all my might. Come on God, she has more to do for you, she has her unborn grandchild to cradle and

Rebirth

this book to read. Still, God was calling her home. We grieve them but I do not think they grieve leaving. We beg people to stay on Earth. Yet, I wonder is it better for them to be welcomed into their new body in heaven? I begged for more time, that time was not granted. I have learned in my life that God's ways are not our ways. He has ordered the day of our birth and the day of our death. Trying to make sense of death is an impossible task. The timing of death will never be the right time. The only part of death that is good, is that the one we have 'lost' is not lost but forever at home in heaven.

My life is mourning the loss of such an inspirational, heavenly warrior. It hurts. It broke me into pieces. It breaks me every time I hear her name, Grace. I couldn't imagine completing this book unless she was here to read it from cover to cover, until one day, I found an email from her. I had sent a few paragraphs of my writing for her to sample. Her reply to those words will follow. But what is so sad is that she wanted to write her own book and her words are far more gifted than mine.

Dear Annabel,
Birthing is painful and your are birthing this book with no gas and air, but by the Holy Spirit. Birthing something so wonderful it will free the captive, deliver children in abuse and neglect and touch the lives of those you never imagined.

The verse from the Bible I gift to your Little One. Isaiah 58:8,11 and 12 "And your ancient ruins shall be rebuilt, you shall raise up the foundations of many generations. You shall be called the repairer of the breach, the restorer of the streets to dwell in."

I hope my not-so-little hands can manage even a fraction of this. For you, for us, for them, I have tried. I never lifted my pen to seek revenge. I lifted my pen in the pursuit of freedom from snow globe living. My snow globe glass hasn't shattered, rather I lift the key I have found. It is painted in grace and covered in forgiveness.

The snow stops, the shaking stops. I stop. In my mind I play a Christian Spanish song, by Marco Barrientos *Me Sanaste Con Tu Bien*. In English this translates as 'you heal me with your good'. No description can describe it. I am falling deeper and deeper into his arms. In you Jesus my shame is evaporating, melting to slush. For now, I try to focus my attention to God's promises and the knowledge that he will never leave or forsake me. This cannot be changed by the wind of circumstances, the flood of emotions, or the evil in others.

My God deliver me from all anger, bitterness and hopelessness. May I make the conscious decision to forgive everyday. Forgiveness is difficult and at times I may fail but still I will try until I can say, "Thank you for my wounds as they have made me a more compassionate adult." I have been angry with the Church, with government legislation and grown-ups.

Rebirth

My call for reform remains, but I release my anger, I let go of my bitterness and accept that my story reads as it does. I see my pain was permitted and perhaps for the greater good of humanity.

I exchange my bitterness for multiplied empathy for others in pain. I squash my temptation to think that parts of my life are hopeless. I invite hope into every single line of the story of my life. I spray my own handmade perfume onto my skin, Hold on to Hope. I allow my mind to be drenched in the love that has been poured into my life since conception. Why did I not spray this again before now? I had this bottle of cologne the whole time, but made the unconscious decision to let go of hope instead. I think this is the default setting of the human heart. It is easier to let go of hope than hold on to it during difficult seasons when hope is deferred and all seems lost.

I allowed myself to use my adult body as my cocoon and all that is left of her is a pile of dead skin. I wear it as a scarf, I look in the mirror and whisper, "Hello Annabel, this is your rebirth." It feels emotional to wear this scarf, it smells of a womb that once worked, a successful teacher, and a scent of a life that is no longer. My adult body had to die just as the caterpillar does. This rebirth was painful. In fact, the pain was so intense that the writing was delayed time after time. That increased the pain as it felt like the onlookers could not understand why it was taking Little One so long to finish the writing. If the truth be told, these 18 chapters were written quickly, but I was left to watch

Little One's Whisper

my adult body endure so much opposition, that it took five years to complete it. She was stripped of everything. So how long did it take me to write this book? The easiest answer is that it took me 'a day and a lifetime.'

I was so tempted to abort this book and the evil one tried to convince me that no one would ever benefit from this book. However, I raise my little voice and say the last section of the Lord's Prayer aloud, "And lead us not into temptation but deliver us from evil, for thine is the kingdom the power and the glory for ever and ever. Amen."

I was flirting with temptation even though I am aware of John 10:10 "The thief comes only to kill steal and destroy. I came that they may have life and have it abundantly." Still, temptation lures me as what God is asking me to do through my book is not what I want. Not everything we desire leads to freedom though. The freedom the world offers is, in reality, false. Stop hurting your Alma searching for love in this empty world. I made myself a human hypothesis to say with certainty that the love you crave is found In Jesus. Self-sacrificing, unconditional, unchanging, passionate, forgiving, gracious and pure.

Preparing to lay down my pen evokes grief within me. I thought at times that writing was difficult. I was wrong, what pains me the most now is letting go of my secrets that were once unwritten. Even whispering them onto pages sounds too loud. There is no triumphant call to celebrate, rather I grieve my privacy.

Rebirth

I wish I could put this writing on the fire. I would happily celebrate if that was the case. I'd share the words with a few close friends, toast marshmallows and happily open that bottle of champagne, that life of late has not required in any act of celebration. I doubt myself; I doubt my intentions. I do not want to cause any pain to Dad, Hands or offend the Church by my honest reviews.

I actually hope there is healing in those relationships. I want to help them. I accept they have untreated grief, wounds and hurts. I hope this book helps them to be free one day too. I really do. Still, I want to hide my words. I'm scared, very scared.

As I sit here today, never could I have imagined the day I first penned my words, when I invited my emotions to the forefront of my conscious thinking – when I accepted my snow globe conditions as reality. Never could I imagine that you, my reader, would be placed in your own snow globe this past year and counting. Not through the same invitation that writing this book demanded of course. Rather through the global pandemic of Covid-19. Country upon country forced into lockdown. Humans shut off from contact in tangible form. Perhaps lockdown living allows you to fully identify with me Little One.

Only in this temporary encasing of your own snow globe conditions can you fully imagine my frustrations; there are few distractions from pain in this isolated state. Social media and online shopping beg for attention. It is hard to hide from yourself in lockdown,

Little One's Whisper

the stillness allows you to hear the whisper, "Where do you hurt?" You cannot numb the void with holidays, parties and theatre trips. If you wait, quite often you hear the echo, "I know you hurt". I know your hurt in places that you pretend to the world that they are not raw. There is a temptation in the snow globe to draw the curtains of your mind and busy yourself, DIY has never been so popular. Yet I wonder who has been willing and ready to deconstruct and rebuild their inner world?

Yet lockdown, if you let it, becomes a mirror. What do you hide from? Coronavirus has cost lives and unleashed devastation and I imagine the long-term damage will impact society for many years to come. Coronavirus has also welcomed the opportunity to address our lifestyle before the decisions we make eat at our flesh without apology. I imagine by the time this book is published that this lockdown will have been lifted. But the future long-term remains uncertain. I think if another lockdown returns, we should stop and reflect how many of us settle for less in the fear of being alone? I wonder, like Little One, how many of us have a virus running through our veins from years of negative words being spoken over us? Do you not see this type of thinking is way more paralysing than lockdown; we are prisoners of our own minds when we accept this as truth?

So, I wonder as I journey to book's completion will you join me and allow yourself to enter the snow globe of change. There is always room for changes for the better, legally, through policy and relationships. It hurts. I wish someone had warned me how badly it would hurt to tend to my wounds. I would never send a postcard saying wish you were here, but at the same time, by surrendering to the snow globe, healing can occur. So, I do not legally instruct you to stay at home, rather I say stay with me I'd rather like the company. At times I catch myself longing for life to go back to normal, but then I see our 'normal' was sick, the world was unwell long before Covid-19, racism, homelessness, extremism, economic disparity, inequality, poverty. The list goes on, and on, and on. Come on, I wonder if God is giving us an opportunity not to return to normal.

Covid has shone a floodlight on the extensive illness in societies "Norms" and we normalised these sick standards "Normal" should never be where we go back to. We need normality in the sense of hugs and connection. But on another level the world values are poorly. The education system is now as target driven as a sales team. The crime rate is rising, and children are struggling to eat as the government offers them scraps. We do not want normal; we need a revival of love. I guess to heal this ailing world, we need Jesus alongside this vaccine. A vaccine can deal with the virus, but the terminal illness of our world needs Jesus to save it. I am not talking about religion I am talking about a personal relationship with God. A God that loves us all and is whispering to your soul to feel its worth, to really feel its worth and be set free. I unlock my snow globe and take a step of faith ... who knows what will happen now?

Little One's Whisper

I say in totality for the first time in my life:
Our Father, who art in heaven,
Hallowed be thy name;
Thy kingdom come;
Thy will be done,
On earth as it is in heaven.
Give us this day our daily bread,
And forgive us our trespasses as we forgive those who trespass against us,
And lead us not into temptation,
But deliver us from evil,
For thine is the kingdom, the power and the glory,
Forever and ever.
Amen. (Matthew 6:9-15)

Padre nuestro,
que estás en el cielo.
Santificado sea tu nombre.
Venga tu reino.
Hágase tu voluntad en la tierra como en el cielo.
Danos hoy nuestro pan de cada día.
Perdona nuestras ofensas,
como también nosotros perdonamos a los que nos ofenden.
No nos dejes caer en tentación y líbranos del mal.
Amén.

*

Rebirth

I hope I can write to you again one day and let you know what I am up to. My conclusion is ironic. I started this writing with the grief of losing my mother and I end this book with the grief of losing Grace. However, I can promise you that grief does not have to condemn you to snow globe living forever. It is important to enter the snow globe and face grief. Whether that grief be the death of a loved one, childhood trauma, divorce, redundancy, whatever pains you – face it.

I thought living in a snow globe was a prison, but the time I spent in the snow globe facing all my hurt and pain has in fact been the medicine I needed. One thing I maintain is that no child should ever be placed inside a snow globe. Oh, I know in this life they cannot be immune to death, sadness, disease and family breakdowns; however, they can be guided through these experiences with love and compassion. If only grown-ups could see the world through the eyes of a helpless child. I could not smash my snow globe as a child, but I hold the key as an adult to unlock it. Yet I would rather not have been placed in a situation where I needed to hold a key.

We must help children to smash out of their snow globe living, so they never have to pick up a key in adult life. Since I began to write Rebirth, the only private disabled overnight provision in Northern Ireland has now been sold. We cannot continue to allow disabled people to live in snow globes, I want to change this. Will you help me?

Hotels advertise that they have disabled facilities. Do

not be fooled. This provision is quite often inadequate. Many disabled people require more than a tokenistic shower rail. They need ceiling hoists and adapted beds, why are we permitting this discrimination?

This is not normal. Come on, open your eyes Northern Ireland!

I unravel my adult scars from round my neck and pull it away from my 2 C-section scars from my gynae surgery. Only now do I see the symbolism in 2 scars. One from the rebirth of Dolly. One for the rebirth of Little One. I weep, I have grown so accustomed to having my adult body's skin. I am conditioned to snow globe living. How will I let go? I too am aware that freedom is not going to come easily, being encased in a snow globe has allowed negative thoughts to form and these will need breaking when they reappear in my weak moments. I pick up a Polaroid camera and begin to take photos of inside my snow globe. This seems crazy. I have been desperate to escape this dome, but I have also grown used to this place. It is difficult to let go of the familiar, even when that is the very thing that creates entrapment.

I throw the camera to the side. Instead, I call Angelito, robin bird, and the butterflies to follow me. I pick a bunch of snowdrops and kiss goodbye to my glow-worm. I pack up a zip and seal bagful of ice cubes, after all, I am ever hopeful that I am ready to meet summer. It can become familiar to hold onto pain and believe parts of me deserve to be punished. I reject this notion. Alma and Sofia, please can you both hold my hand and drag my body to God's arms.

Rebirth

I unlock the snow globe door with healing and the understanding I have now grasped. I kiss goodbye to the scarf one last time and thank it for its sacrifice. I leave this scarf of skin in my snow globe to decompose. The life I was knew in her body is now over. I am not going to require it any more though, as I am letting go. I am no longer a slave to fear, chained up in silence. The time has arrived to take my first steps as a rebirthed adult. I only own two suitcases, a banger of a car. I rent a single room in a house which is now for sale. I suspect soon I will have to say goodbye to my furry companion Fizzy who resides there too. I have no permanent job as of yet, very little money in my pocket, still I take my first steps in faith. I do not have my own home; I no longer even have my snow globe. Yet, I have my faith and am secure in my identity. Adopted by God into his family, and his skin can fix skin: 2 Corinthians 6:18 "And I will be a Father to you, and you will be my sons and daughters, says the Lord Almighty."

I am going to miss you, my reader, and very much thank you for hearing my Little One's Whisper as I laid my most vital organ onto paper. My very own heart. I miss your brown eyes Anne as you carefully and tenderly listened to my every word.

Snow, snow, snow, shake, shake, I hope this story helps other's glass domes break! Are you ready to whisper your little one to others? Or be adopted into the family of God? Religion, and church attendance has many values too within our society. May we be mindful that above the ceremony and tradition, James 1:27

"Religion that God our Father accepts as pure and faultless is this: to look after orphans and widows in their distress and to keep oneself from being polluted by the world."

Always remember that you deserve more than snow globe living. Let us destroy snow globe homes, neighbourhoods and cities. For you, for us, for them, "Let us smash glass and allow people to feel Summer." Ideally, leaving the smell of the ocean on their skin, and sand between their toes.

Acknowledgements

Where do I begin? The process of bringing this book so far took me five years. During those five years I have been very touched by the kindness of strangers. These people I cannot thank by name, but I am very grateful to them. Never underestimate the power of showing kindness to a stranger.

Thanks to Fizzy the dog for keeping me company, I will never love another dog quite like you.

Huge gratitude to all my friends and ex-colleagues who believed in me and opened their hearts and homes. There are too many of you to mention by name, but for my Spanish, English and Northern Irish friends, gracias. In particular, I thank from the depths of my soul my gaggle. I love you all.

Thanks to my beautiful friend Caroline who typed my book as I dictated my bad handwriting with plenty of coffee. Thank you to my godchildren, Mia and Nathan, for drawing me two beautiful butterflies for my book. I love you to the moon and back.

Thank you to the NHS staff who worked tirelessly to fix my body.

I would like to thank my counsellor Anne Aitken (BACP accredited/Masters in Counselling) 27 years of NHS experience, who is now in private practice. Thank you for going above and beyond the call of duty to help me birth this book. You were my midwife, never failing to

Acknowledgements

firmly grip onto deliverance for Little One. You are simply the kindest person I have ever met, offering free sessions when my finances were too low. PS Dios te bendiga. Little One is full of admiration for you, and your talented work. We simply say, "Nosotras te amamos."

Special thanks to the Burfitts, and Evans and Green families for the loving shelter in their homes in England.

Thanks latterly to my new friends who cheered me across the finishing line. Anne and Mike, and my sewing bees.

Everything in *Little One's Whisper* was a gift from God. The name, the plot, the characters. None of it is mine to claim. I simply am sharing this 'gift 'from God to me to others.

Thank you to Julie Rowlandson for my internal illustration and to Dawn Summerlin for my book cover and for gifting your work to me. Please support their work on Etsy. Julie Rowlandson art elephant on Etsy and Dawn Summerlin perceptive beauty. I hope their free-will offering gains them financial reward from others.

Lastly, but not least, may I thank Rachel and the team from The Choir Press self-publishing company.

Little One's Whisper is dedicated to my friend Grace. I am so sad you never got to read it, but because of you I was determined to publish it. This book is also dedicated to Grace's daughter Dorothy – the wee sister I never had, who is now pregnant with her own little one. May I hold both your hearts all my days.

Acknowledgements

This book is gifted to Dolly. Te quiero tanto, Dolly. The proceeds of this book will go to Dolly. I want to build her a home, so please support Little One in this quest. In due course merchandise such as cards, mugs and pictures will be available on my website. I have other ideas too for the webpage, so watch this space. The webpage is currently still to be built, but it will be named under my book title, and/or name. There will also be a donation option for 'Dolly's House', which I hope will shelter many souls in need and not just her. Hopefully, I can write blogs there and keep you informed of our journey.

Above all, my gratitude is to God who was and continues to be my strength.

Lightning Source UK Ltd.
Milton Keynes UK
UKHW010830110122
396962UK00002B/218

9 781789 632408